# *An Appeal to the Christian Women of the South*

*Angelina Emily Grimke*

# Contents

APPEAL TO THE CHRISTIAN WOMEN OF THE SOUTH ......................7

# AN APPEAL TO THE CHRISTIAN WOMEN OF THE SOUTH

BY
Angelina Emily Grimke

# APPEAL TO THE CHRISTIAN WOMEN OF THE SOUTH

## BY A.E. GRIMKE.

"Then Mordecai commanded to answer Esther, Think not within thyself that thou shalt escape in the king's house more than all the Jews. For if thou altogether holdest thy peace at this time, then shall there enlargement and deliverance arise to the Jews from another place: but thou and thy father's house shall be destroyed: and who knoweth whether thou art come to the kingdom for such a time as this. And Esther bade them return Mordecai this answer:--and so will I go in unto the king, which is not according to law, and if I perish, I perish." Esther IV. 13-16.

Respected Friends,

It is because I feel a deep and tender interest in your present and eternal welfare that I am willing thus publicly to address you. Some of you have loved me as a relative, and some have felt bound to me in Christian sympathy, and Gospel fellowship; and even when compelled by a strong sense of duty, to break those outward bonds of union which bound us together as members of the same community, and members of the same religious denomination, you were generous enough to give me credit, for sincerity as a Christian, though you believed I had been most strangely deceived. I thanked you then for your kindness, and I ask you *now*, for the sake of former confidence, and former friendship, to read the following pages in the spirit of calm investigation and fervent prayer. It is because you have known me, that I write thus unto you.

But there are other Christian women scattered over the Southern States, a very large number of whom have never seen me, and never heard my name, and who feel *no* interest whatever in *me*. But I feel an interest in *you*, as branches of the same vine from whose root I daily draw the principle of spiritual vitality--Yes! Sisters in Christ I feel an interest in *you*, and often has the secret prayer arisen on your behalf, Lord "open thou their eyes that they may see wondrous things out of thy Law"--It is then, because I do feel and do pray for you, that I thus address you upon a subject about which of all others, perhaps you would rather not hear any thing; but, "would to God ye could bear with me a little in my folly, and indeed bear with me, for I am jealous over you with godly jealousy." Be not afraid then to read my appeal; it is *not* written in the heat of passion or prejudice, but in that solemn calmness which is the result of conviction and duty. It is true, I am going to tell you unwelcome truths, but I mean to speak those truths in love, and remember Solomon says, "faithful are the *wounds* of a friend." I do not believe the time has yet come when Christian women "will not endure sound doctrine," even on the subject of Slavery, if it is spoken to them in tenderness and love, therefore I now address *you*.

To all of you then, known or unknown, relatives or strangers, (for you are all *one* in Christ,) I would speak. I have felt for you at this time, when unwelcome light is pouring in upon the world on the subject of slavery; light which even Christians would exclude, if they could, from our country, or at any rate from the southern portion of it, saying, as its rays strike the rock bound coasts of New England and scatter their warmth and radiance over her hills and valleys, and from thence travel onward over the Palisades of the Hudson, and down the soft flowing waters of the Delaware and gild the waves of the Potomac, "hitherto shalt thou come and no further;" I know that even professors of His name who has been emphatically called the "Light of the world" would, if they could, build a wall of adamant around the Southern States whose top might reach unto heaven, in order to shut out the light which is bounding from mountain to mountain and from the hills to the plains and valleys beneath, through the vast extent of our Northern States. But believe me, when I tell you, their attempts will be as utterly fruitless as were the efforts of the builders of Babel; and why? Because moral, like natural light, is so extremely subtle in its nature as to overleap all human barriers, and laugh at the puny efforts of man to control it. All the excuses and palliations of this system must inevitably be swept away, just as other "refuges of lies" have been, by the irresistible torrent of a rectified public opinion. "The *supporters* of the slave system," says Jonathan Dymond in his admirable work on the Principles of Morality, "will *hereafter* be regarded with the *same* public feeling, as he who was an advocate for the slave trade now is." It will be, and that very soon, clearly perceived and fully acknowledged by all the virtuous and the candid, that in *principle* it is as sinful to hold a human being in bondage who has been born in Carolina, as one who has been born in Africa. All that sophistry of argument which has been employed to prove, that although it is sinful to send to Africa to procure men and women as slaves, who have never been in slavery, that still, it is not sinful to keep those in bondage who have come down by inheritance, will be utterly overthrown. We must come back to the good old doctrine of our forefathers who declared to the world, "this self evident truth that *all* men are created equal, and that they have certain *inalienable* rights among which are life, *liberty*, and the pursuit of happiness." It is even a greater absurdity to suppose a man can be legally born a slave under our free Republican Government, than under the petty despotisms of barbarian Africa. If then, we have no right to enslave an African, surely we can have none to enslave an American; if it is a self evident truth that *all* men, every where and of every color are born equal, and have an inalienable right to liberty, then it is equally true that *no* man can be born a slave, and no man can ever *rightfully* be reduced to *involuntary* bondage and held as a slave, however fair may be the claim of his master or mistress through wills and title-deeds.

But after all, it may be said, our fathers were certainly mistaken, for the Bible sanctions Slavery, and that is the highest authority. Now the Bible is my ultimate appeal in all matters of faith and practice, and it is to this test I am anxious to bring the subject at issue between us. Let us then begin with Adam and examine the charter of privileges which was given to him. "Have dominion over the fish of the sea, and over the fowl of the air, and over every living thing that moveth upon the earth." In the eighth Psalm we have a still fuller description of this charter which through Adam was given to all mankind. "Thou madest him to have dominion over the works of thy hands; thou hast put all things under his feet. All sheep and oxen, yea, and the beasts of the field, the fowl of the air, the fish of the sea, and whatsoever passeth through the paths of the seas." And after the flood when this charter of human rights was renewed, we find no additional power vested in man. "And the fear of you and the dread of you shall be upon every beast of the earth, and every fowl of the air, and upon all that moveth upon the earth, and upon all the fishes of the sea, into your hand are they delivered." In this charter, although the different kinds of *irrational* beings are so particularly enumerated, and supreme dominion over all of them is granted, yet *man* is *never* vested with this dominion over his fellow man; he was never told that any of the human species were put under his feet; it was only all things, and man, who was created in the image of his Maker, *never* can properly be termed a *thing*, though the laws of Slave States do call him "a chattel personal;" *Man* then, I assert *never* was put under the feet of man, by that first charter of human rights which was given by God, to the Fathers of the Antediluvian and Postdiluvian worlds, therefore this doctrine of equality is based on the Bible.

But it may be argued, that in the very chapter of Genesis from which I have last quoted, will be found the curse pronounced upon Canaan, by which his posterity was consigned to servitude under his brothers Shem and Japheth. I know this prophecy was uttered, and was most fearfully and wonderfully fulfilled, through the immediate descendants of Canaan, i.e. the Canaanites, and I do not know but it has been through all the children of Ham but I do know that prophecy does *not* tell us what ought to be, but what actually does take place, ages after it has been delivered, and that if we justify America for enslaving the children of Africa, we must also justify Egypt for reducing the children of Israel to bondage, for the latter was foretold as explicitly as the former. I am well aware that prophecy has often been urged as an excuse for Slavery, but be not deceived, the fulfilment of prophecy will not cover one sin in the awful day of account. Hear what our Saviour says on this subject; "it must needs be that offences come, but woe unto that man through whom they come"--Witness some fulfilment of this declaration in the tremendous destruction, of Jerusalem, occasioned by that most nefarious of all crimes the crucifixion of the Son of God. Did the fact of that event having been foretold, exculpate the Jews from sin in perpetrating it; No--for hear what the Apostle Peter says to them on this subject, "Him being delivered by the determinate counsel and foreknowledge of God, *ye* have taken, and by *wicked* hands have crucified and slain."

Other striking instances might be adduced, but these will suffice.

But it has been urged that the patriarchs held slaves, and therefore, slavery is right. Do you really believe that patriarchal servitude was like American slavery? Can you believe it? If so, read the history of these primitive fathers of the church and be undeceived. Look at Abraham, though so great a man, going to the herd himself and fetching a calf from thence and serving it up with his own hands, for the entertainment of his guests. Look at Sarah, that princess as her name signifies, baking cakes upon the hearth. If the servants they had were like Southern slaves, would they have performed such comparatively menial offices for themselves? Hear too the plaintive lamentation of Abraham when he feared he should have no son to bear his name down to posterity. "Behold thou hast given me no seed, &c, one born in my house is mine heir." From this it appears that one of his ***servants*** was to inherit his immense estate. Is this like Southern slavery? I leave it to your own good sense and candor to decide. Besides, such was the footing upon which Abraham was with ***his*** servants, that he trusted them with arms. Are slaveholders willing to put swords and pistols into the hands of their slaves? He was as a father among his servants; what are planters and masters generally among theirs? When the institution of circumcision was established, Abraham was commanded thus; "He that is eight days old shall be circumcised among you, ***every*** man-child in your generations; he that is born in the house, or bought with money of any stranger which is not of thy seed." And to render this command with regard to his ***servants*** still more impressive it is repeated in the very next verse; and herein we may perceive the great care which was taken by God to guard the rights of servants even under this "dark dispensation." What too was the testimony given to the faithfulness of this eminent patriarch. "For I know him that he will command his children and his ***household*** after him, and they shall keep the way of the Lord to do justice and judgment." Now my dear friends many of you believe that circumcision has been superseded by baptism in the Church; Are you careful to have ***all*** that are born in your house or bought with money of any stranger, baptized? Are ***you*** as faithful as Abraham to command your household to keep the way of the Lord? I leave it to your own consciences to decide. Was patriarchal servitude then like American Slavery?

But I shall be told, God sanctioned Slavery, yea commanded Slavery under the Jewish Dispensation. Let us examine this subject calmly and prayerfully. I admit that a species of *servitude* was permitted to the Jews, but in studying the subject I have been struck with wonder and admiration at perceiving how carefully the servant was guarded from violence, injustice and wrong. I will first inform you how these servants became servants, for I think this a very important part of our subject. From consulting Horne, Calmet and the Bible, I find there were six different ways by which the Hebrews became servants legally.

1. If reduced to extreme poverty, a Hebrew might sell himself, i.e. his services, for six years, in which case *he* received the purchase money *himself*. Lev. xxv, 39.

2. A father might sell his children as servants, i.e. his *daughters*, in which circumstance it was understood the daughter was to be the wife or daughter-in-law of the man who bought her, and the *father* received the price. In other words, Jewish women were sold as white women were in the first settlement of Virginia-- as *wives*, *not* as slaves. Ex. xxi, 7.

3. Insolvent debtors might be delivered to their creditors as servants. 2 Kings iv, 1

4. Thieves not able to make restitution for their thefts, were sold for the benefit of the injured person. Ex. xxii, 3.

5. They might be born in servitude. Ex. xxi, 4.

6. If a Hebrew had sold himself to a rich Gentile, he might be redeemed by one of his brethren at any time the money was offered; and he who redeemed him, was *not* to take advantage of the favor thus conferred, and rule over him with rigor. Lev. xxv, 47-55.

Before going into an examination of the laws by which these servants were protected, I would just ask whether American slaves have become slaves in any of the ways in which the Hebrews became servants. Did they sell themselves into slavery and receive the purchase money into their own hands? No! Did they become insolvent, and by their own imprudence subject themselves to be sold as slaves? No! Did they steal the property of another, and were they sold to make restitution for their crimes? No! Did their present masters, as an act of kindness, redeem them from some heathen tyrant to whom they had sold themselves in the dark hour of adversity? No! Were they born in slavery? No! No! not according to Jewish Law, for the servants who were born in servitude among them, were born of parents who had sold themselves for six years: Ex. xxi, 4. Were the female slaves of the South sold by their fathers? How shall I answer this question? Thousands and tens of thousands never were, *their* fathers *never* have received the poor compensation of silver or gold for the tears and toils, the suffering, and anguish, and hopeless bondage of *their* daughters. They labor day by day, and year by year, side by side, in the same field, if haply their daughters are permitted to remain on the same plantation with them, instead of being as they often are, separated from their parents and sold into distant states, never again to meet on earth. But do the fathers of the South ever sell their daughters? My heart beats, and my hand trembles, as I write the awful affirmative, Yes! The fathers of this Christian land often sell their daughters, *not* as Jewish parents did, to be the wives and daughters-in-law of the man who buys them, but to be the abject slaves of petty tyrants and irresponsible masters. Is it not so, my friends? I leave it to your own candor to corroborate my assertion. Southern slaves then have *not* become slaves in any of the six different ways in which Hebrews became servants, and I hesitate not to say that American masters *cannot* according to Jewish law substantiate their claim to the men, women, or children they now hold in bondage.

But there was one way in which a Jew might illegally be reduced to servitude; it was this, he might be *stolen* and afterwards sold as a slave, as was Joseph. To guard most effectually against this dreadful crime of manstealing, God enacted this severe law. "He that stealeth a man and selleth him, or if he be found in his hand, he shall surely be put to death." [1] As I have tried American Slavery by *legal* Hebrew servitude, and found, (to your surprise, perhaps,) that Jewish law cannot justify the slaveholder's claim, let us now try it by *illegal* Hebrew bondage. Have the Southern slaves then been, stolen? If they did not sell themselves into bondage; if they were not sold as insolvent debtors or as thieves; if they were not redeemed from a heathen master to whom they had sold themselves; if they were not born in servitude according to Hebrew law; and if the females were not sold by their fathers as wives and daughters-in-law to those who purchased them; then what shall we say of them? what can we say of them but that according to Hebrew Law they have been stolen.

But I shall be told that the Jews had other servants who were absolute slaves. Let us look a little into this also. They had other servants who were procured in two different ways.

1. Captives taken in war were reduced to bondage instead of being killed; but we are not told that their children were enslaved Deut. xx, 14.

2. Bondmen and bondmaids might be bought from the heathen round about them; these were left by fathers to their children after them, but it does not appear that the ***children*** of these servants ever were reduced to servitude. Lev. xxv, 44.

I will now try the right of the southern planter by the claims of Hebrew masters over their ***heathen*** slaves. Were the southern slaves taken captive in war? No! Were they bought from the heathen? No! for surely, no one will ***now*** vindicate the slave-trade so far as to assert that slaves were bought from the heathen who were obtained by that system of piracy. The ***only*** excuse for holding southern slaves is that they were born in slavery, but we have seen that they were ***not*** born in servitude as Jewish servants were, and that the children of heathen slaves were not legally subjected to bondage even under the Mosaic Law. How then have the slaves of the South been obtained?

I will next proceed to an examination of those laws which were enacted in order to protect the Hebrew and the Heathen servant; for I wish you to understand that ***both*** are protected by Him, of whom it is said "his mercies are over ***all*** his works." I will first speak of those which secured the rights of Hebrew servants. This code was headed thus:

1. Thou shalt ***not*** rule over him with ***rigor***, but shalt fear thy God;

2. If thou buy a Hebrew servant, six years shall he serve, and in the seventh year he shall go out free for nothing. Ex. xxi, 2. [2]

3. If he come in by himself, he shall go out by himself; if he were married, then his wife shall go out with him.

4. If his master have given him a wife and she have borne him sons and daughters, the wife and her children shall be his master's, and he shall go out by himself.

5. If the servant shall plainly say, I love my master, my wife, and my children; I will not go out free; then his master shall bring him unto the Judges, and he shall bring him to the door, or unto the door-post, and his master shall bore his ear through with an awl, and he shall serve him ***forever***. Ex. xxi, 5-6.

6. If a man smite the eye of his servant, or the eye of his maid, that it perish, he shall let him go ***free*** for his eye's sake. And if he smite out his man servant's tooth

or his maid servant's tooth, he shall let him go *free* for his tooth's sake. Ex. xxi, 26, 27.

7. On the Sabbath rest was secured to servants by the fourth commandment. Ex. xx, 10.

8. Servants were permitted to unite with their masters three times in every year in celebrating the Passover, the feast of Pentecost, and the feast of Tabernacles; every male throughout the land was to appear before the Lord at Jerusalem with a gift; here the bond and the free stood on common ground. Deut. xvi.

9. If a man smite his servant or his maid with a rod, and he die under his hand, he shall be surely punished. Notwithstanding, if he continue a day or two, he shall not be punished, for he is his money. Ex. xxi, 20, 21.

From these laws we learn that Hebrew men servants were bound to serve their masters only six years, unless their attachment to their employers their wives and children, should induce them to wish to remain in servitude, in which case, in order to prevent the possibility of deception on the part of the master, the servant was first taken before the magistrate, where he openly declared his intention of continuing in his master's service, (probably a public register was kept of such) he was then conducted to the door of the house, (in warm climates doors are thrown open,) and *there* his ear was *publicly* bored, and by submitting to this operation he testified his willingness to serve him *forever*, i.e. during his life, for Jewish Rabbins who must have understood Jewish *slavery*, (as it is called,) "affirm that servants were set free at the death of their masters and did *not* descend to their heirs:" or that he was to serve him until the year of Jubilee, when *all* servants were set at liberty. To protect servants from violence, it was ordained that if a master struck out the tooth or destroyed the eye of a servant, that servant immediately became *free*, for such an act of violence evidently showed he was unfit to possess the power of a master, and therefore that power was taken from him. All servants enjoyed the rest of the Sabbath and partook of the privileges and festivities of the three great Jewish Feasts; and if a servant died under the infliction of chastisement, his master was surely to be punished. As a tooth for a tooth and life for life was the Jewish law, of course he was punished with death. I know that great stress has been laid upon the following verse: "Notwithstanding, if he continue a day or two, he shall not be punished, for he is his money."

Slaveholders, and the apologists of slavery, have eagerly seized upon this little passage of scripture, and held it up as the masters' Magna Charta, by which they were licensed by God himself to commit the greatest outrages upon the defenceless victims of their oppression. But, my friends, was it designed to be so? If our Heavenly Father would protect by law the eye and the tooth of a Hebrew servant, can we for a moment believe that he would abandon that same servant to the brutal rage of a master who would destroy even life itself. Do we not rather see in this, the ***only*** law which protected masters, and was it not right that in case of the death of a servant, one or two days after chastisement was inflicted, to which other circumstances might have contributed, that the master should be protected when, in all probability, he never intended to produce so fatal a result? But the phrase "he is his money" has been adduced to show that Hebrew servants were regarded as mere ***things***, "chattels personal;" if so, why were so many laws made to secure their rights as men, and to ensure their rising into equality and freedom? If they were mere ***things***, why were they regarded as responsible beings, and one law made for them as well as for their masters? But I pass on now to the consideration of how the ***female*** Jewish servants were protected by ***law***.

1. If she please not her master, who hath betrothed her to himself, then shall he let her be redeemed: to sell her unto another nation he shall have no power, seeing he hath dealt deceitfully with her.

2. If he have betrothed her unto his son, he shall deal with her after the manner of daughters.

3. If he take him another wife, her food, her raiment, and her duty of marriage, shall he not diminish.

4. If he do not these three unto her, then shall she go out ***free*** without money.

On these laws I will give you Calmet's remarks; "A father could not sell his daughter as a slave, according to the Rabbins, until she was at the age of puberty, and unless he were reduced to the utmost indigence. Besides when a master bought an Israelitish girl, it was *always* with the presumption that he would take her to wife. Hence Moses adds, 'if she please not her master, and he does not think fit to marry her, he shall set her at liberty,' or according to the Hebrew, 'he shall let her be redeemed.' 'To sell her to another nation he shall have no power, seeing he hath dealt deceitfully with her;' as to the engagement implied, at least of taking her to wife. 'If he have betrothed her unto his son, he shall deal with her after the manner of daughters, i.e. he shall take care that his son uses her as his wife, that he does not despise or maltreat her. If he make his son marry another wife, he shall give her her dowry, her clothes and compensation for her virginity; if he does none of these three, she shall go out free without money." Thus were the rights of female servants carefully secured by law under the Jewish Dispensation; and now I would ask, are the rights of female slaves at the South thus secured? Are *they* sold only as wives and daughters-in-law, and when not treated as such, are they allowed to go out free? No! They have *all* not only been illegally obtained as servants according to Hebrew law, but they are also illegally **held** in bondage. Masters at the South and West have all forfeited their claims, (if they ever had any,) to their female slaves.

We come now to examine the case of those servants who were "of the heathen round about;" Were *they* left entirely unprotected by law? Horne in speaking of the law, "Thou shalt not rule over him with rigor, but shall fear thy God," remarks, "this law Lev. xxv, 43, it is true speaks expressly of slaves who were of Hebrew descent; but as alien born slaves were ingrafted into the Hebrew Church by circumcision, there is no doubt but that it applied to *all* slaves;" if so, then we may reasonably suppose that the other protective laws extended to them also; and that the only difference between Hebrew and Heathen servants lay in this, that the former served but six years unless they chose to remain longer, and were always freed at the death of their masters; whereas the latter served until the year of Jubilee, though that might include a period of forty-nine years,--and were left from father to son.

There are however two other laws which I have not yet noticed. The one effectually prevented all involuntary servitude, and the other completely abolished Jewish servitude every fifty years. They were equally operative upon the Heathen and the Hebrew.

1. "Thou shall *not* deliver unto his master the servant that is escaped from his master unto thee. He shall dwell with thee, even among you, in that place which he shall choose, in one of thy gates where it liketh him best: thou shall *not* oppress him." Deut. xxiii, 15, 16.

2. "And ye shall hallow the fiftieth year, and proclaim *Liberty* throughout *all*

the land, unto *all* the inhabitants thereof: it shall be a jubilee unto you." Lev. xxv, 10.

Here, then, we see that by this first law, the door of Freedom was opened wide to every servant who had any cause whatever for complaint; if he was unhappy with his master, all he had to do was to leave him, and no man had a right to deliver him back to him again, and not only so, but the absconded servant was to *choose* where he should live, and no Jew was permitted to oppress him. He left his master just as our Northern servants leave us; we have no power to compel them to remain with us, and no man has any right to oppress them; they go and dwell in that place where it chooseth them, and live just where they like. Is it so at the South? Is the poor runaway slave protected by law from the violence of that master whose oppression and cruelty has driven him from his plantation or his house? No! no! Even the free states of the North are compelled to deliver unto his master the servant that is escaped from his master into them. By *human* law, under the Christian Dispensation, in the nineteenth century we are commanded to do, what **God** more than three thousand years ago, under the Mosaic Dispensation, positively commanded the Jews *not* to do. In the wide domain even of our free states, there is not *one* city of refuge for the poor runaway fugitive; not one spot upon which he can stand and say, I am a free man--I am protected in my rights as a *man*, by the strong arm of the law; no! not one. How long the North will thus shake hands with the South in sin, I know not. How long she will stand by like the persecutor Saul, *consenting* unto the death of Stephen, and keeping the raiment of them that slew him. I know not; but one thing I do know, the guilt of the North is increasing in a tremendous ratio as light is pouring in upon her on the subject and the sin of slavery. As the sun of righteousness climbs higher and higher in the moral heavens, she will stand still more and more abashed as the query is thundered down into her ear, "*Who* hath required *this* at thy hand?" It will be found *no* excuse then that the Constitution of our country required that persons bound to service escaping from their masters should be delivered up; no more excuse than was the reason which Adam assigned for eating the forbidden fruit. *He* was condemned and punished because he hearkened to the voice of his wife, rather than to the command of his Maker; and *we* will assuredly be condemned and punished for obeying *Man* rather than ***God***, if we do not speedily repent and bring forth fruits meet for repentance. Yea, are we not receiving chastisement even ***now***?

But by the second of these laws a still more astonishing fact is disclosed. If the first effectually prevented all involuntary servitude, the last absolutely forbade even voluntary servitude being perpetual. On the great day of atonement every fiftieth year the Jubilee trumpet was sounded throughout the land of Judea, and ***Liberty*** was proclaimed to ***all*** the inhabitants thereof. I will not say that the servants' ***chains*** fell off and their ***manacles*** were burst, for there is no evidence that Jewish servants ***ever*** felt the weight of iron chains, and collars, and handcuffs; but I do say that even the man who had voluntarily sold himself and the ***heathen*** who had been sold to a Hebrew master, were set free, the one as well as the other. This law was evidently designed to prevent the oppression of the poor, and the possibility of such a thing as perpetual servitude existing among them.

Where, then, I would ask, is the warrant, the justification, or the palliation of American Slavery from Hebrew servitude? How many of the southern slaves would now be in bondage according to the laws of Moses; Not one. You may observe that I have carefully avoided using the term ***slavery*** when speaking of Jewish servitude; and simply for this reason, that no such thing existed among that people; the word translated servant does ***not*** mean ***slave***, it is the same that is applied to Abraham, to Moses, to Elisha and the prophets generally. Slavery then never existed under the Jewish Dispensation at all, and I cannot but regard it as an aspersion on the character of Him who is "glorious in Holiness" for any one to assert that "God sanctioned, yea commanded slavery under the old dispensation." I would fain lift my feeble voice to vindicate Jehovah's character from so foul a slander. If slaveholders are determined to hold slaves as long as they can, let them not dare to say that the God of mercy and of truth ***ever*** sanctioned such a system of cruelty and wrong. It is blasphemy against Him.

We have seen that the code of laws framed by Moses with regard to servants was designed to protect them as men and women, to secure to them their rights as human beings, to guard them from oppression and defend them from violence of every kind. Let us now turn to the Slave laws of the South and West and examine them too. I will give you the substance only, because I fear I shall tresspass too much on your time, were I to quote them at length.

1. ***Slavery*** is hereditary and perpetual, to the last moment of the slave's earthly existence, and to all his descendants to the latest posterity.

2. The labor of the slave is compulsory and uncompensated; while the kind of labor, the amount of toil, the time allowed for rest, are dictated solely by the master. No bargain is made, no wages given. A pure despotism governs the human brute; and even his covering and provender, both as to quantity and quality, depend entirely on the master's discretion. [3]

3. The slave being considered a personal chattel may be sold or pledged, or leased at the will of his master. He may be exchanged for marketable commodities, or taken in execution for the debts or taxes either of a living or dead master. Sold at auction, either individually, or in lots to suit the purchaser, he may remain with his family, or be separated from them for ever.

4. Slaves can make no contracts and have no ***legal*** right to any property, real or personal. Their own honest earnings and the legacies of friends belong in point of law to their masters.

5. Neither a slave nor a free colored person can be a witness against any ***white***, or free person, in a court of justice, however atrocious may have been the crimes they have seen him commit, if such testimony would be for the benefit of a ***slave***; but they may give testimony against a fellow slave, or free colored man, even in cases affecting life, if the ***master*** is to reap the advantage of it.

6. The slave may be punished at his master's discretion--without trial--without any means of legal redress; whether his offence be real or imaginary; and the master can transfer the same despotic power to any person or persons, he may choose to appoint.

7. The slave is not allowed to resist any free man under ***any*** circumstances, ***his*** only safety consists in the fact that his ***owner*** may bring suit and recover the price of his body, in case his life is taken, or his limbs rendered unfit for labor.

8. Slaves cannot redeem themselves, or obtain a change of masters, though cruel treatment may have' rendered such a change necessary for their personal safety.

9. The slave is entirely unprotected in his domestic relations.

10. The laws greatly obstruct the manumission of slaves, even where the master is willing to enfranchise them.

11. The operation of the laws tends to deprive slaves of religious instruction and consolation.

12. The whole power of the laws is exerted to keep slaves in a state of the lowest ignorance.

13. There is in this country a monstrous inequality of law and right. What is a trifling fault in the white man, is considered highly criminal--in the slave; the same offences which cost a white man a few dollars only, are punished in the negro with death.

14. The laws operate most oppressively upon free people of color. [4] Shall I ask you now my friends, to draw the parallel between Jewish *servitude* and American *slavery*? No! For there is no likeness in the two systems; I ask you rather to mark the contrast. The laws of Moses protected servants in their rights as men and women, guarded them from oppression and defended them from wrong. The Code Noir of the South robs the slave of all his rights as a *man*, reduces him to a chattel personal, and defends the master in the exercise of the most unnatural and unwarrantable power over his slave. They each bear the impress of the hand which formed them. The attributes of justice and mercy are shadowed out in the Hebrew code; those of injustice and cruelty, in the Code Noir of America. Truly it was wise in the slaveholders of the South to declare their slaves to be "chattels personal;" for before they could be robbed of wages, wives, children, and friends, it was absolutely necessary to deny they were human beings. It is wise in them, to keep them in abject ignorance, for the strong man armed must be bound before we can spoil his house--the powerful intellect of man must be bound down with the iron chains of nescience before we can rob him of his rights as a man; we must reduce him to a *thing* before we can claim the right to set our feet upon his neck, because it was only all things which were originally put under the feet of man by the Almighty and Beneficent Father of all, who has declared himself to be no respecter of persons, whether red, white or black.

But some have even said that Jesus Christ did not condemn slavery. To this I reply that our Holy Redeemer lived and preached among the Jews only. The laws which Moses had enacted fifteen hundred years previous to his appearance among them, had never been annulled, and these laws protected every servant in Palestine. If then He did not condemn Jewish servitude this does not prove that he would not have condemned such a monstrous system as that of American *slavery*, if that had existed among them. But did not Jesus condemn slavery? Let us examine some of his precepts. "***Whatsoever*** ye would that men should do to you, do ye even so to them," Let every slaveholder apply these queries to his own heart; Am *I* willing to be a slave--Am *I* willing to see *my* wife the slave of another--Am *I* willing to see my mother a slave, or my father, my sister or my brother? If *not*, then in holding others as slaves, I am doing what I would *not* wish to be done to me or any relative I have; and thus have I broken this golden rule which was given *me* to walk by.

But some slaveholders have said, "we were never in bondage to any man," and therefore the yoke of bondage would be insufferable to us, but slaves are accustomed to it, their backs are fitted to the burden. Well, I am willing to admit that you who have lived in freedom would find slavery even more oppressive than the poor slave does, but then you may try this question in another form--Am I willing to reduce my little child to slavery? You know that if it is brought up a slave it will never know any contrast, between freedom and bondage, its back will become fitted to the burden just as the negro child's does--not by nature--but by daily, violent pressure, in the same way that the head of the Indian child becomes flattened by the boards in which it is bound. It has been justly remarked that "God never made a slave," he made man upright; his back was *not* made to carry burdens, nor his neck to wear a yoke, and the *man* must be crushed within him, before ***his*** back can be ***fitted*** to the burden of perpetual slavery; and that his back is *not* fitted to it, is manifest by the insurrections that so often disturb the peace and security of slaveholding countries. Who ever heard of a rebellion of the beasts of the field; and why not? simply because *they* were all placed under the feet of man, into whose hand they were delivered; it was originally designed that they should serve him, therefore their necks have been formed for the yoke, and their backs for the burden; but not so with man, intellectual, immortal man! I appeal to you, my friends, as mothers; Are you willing to enslave *your* children? You start back with horror and indignation at such a question. But why, if slavery is no wrong to those upon whom it is imposed? why, if as has often been said, slaves are happier than their masters, free from the cares and perplexities of providing for themselves and their families? why not place your children in the way of being supported without your having the trouble to provide for them, or they for themselves? Do you not perceive that as soon as this golden rule of action is applied to *yourselves* that you involuntarily shrink from the test; as soon as *your* actions are weighed in *this* balance of the sanctuary that you are found wanting? Try yourselves by another of the Divine precepts, "Thou shalt love thy neighbor as thyself." Can we love a man *as* we love *ourselves* if we do, and continue to do unto him, what we would not wish any one to do to us? Look too, at Christ's example, what does he say of himself, "I came *not* to be ministered unto, but to minister." Can you for a moment imagine the meek, and lowly, and compassionate Saviour, a *slaveholder*? do you not shudder at this thought as much as at that of his being a warrior? But why, if slavery is not sinful?

Again, it has been said, the Apostle Paul did not condemn Slavery, for he sent Onesimus back to Philemon. I do not think it can be said he sent him back, for no coercion was made use of. Onesimus was not thrown into prison and then sent back in chains to his master, as your runaway slaves often are--this could not possibly have been the case, because you know Paul as a Jew, was bound to protect the runaway, he had no right to send any fugitive back to his master. The state of the case then seems to have been this. Onesimus had been an unprofitable servant to Philemon and left him--he afterwards became converted under the Apostle's preaching, and seeing that he had been to blame in his conduct, and desiring by future fidelity to atone for past error, he wished to return, and the Apostle gave him the letter we now have as a recommendation to Philemon, informing him of the conversion of Onesimus, and entreating him as "Paul the aged" "to receive him, *not* now as a servant, but *above* a servant, a brother beloved, especially to me, but how much more unto thee, both in the flesh and in the Lord. If thou count *me* therefore as a partner, receive him as myself." This then surely cannot be forced into a justification of the practice of returning runaway slaves back to their masters, to be punished with cruel beatings and scourgings as they often are. Besides the word [Greek: doulos] here translated servant, is the same that is made use of in Matt. xviii, 27. Now it appears that this servant owed his lord ten thousand talents; he possessed property to a vast amount. Onesimus could not then have been a *slave*, for slaves do not own their wives, or children; no, not even their own bodies, much less property.

But again, the servitude which the apostle was accustomed to, must have been very different from American slavery, for he says, "the heir (or son), as long as he is a child, differeth nothing from a servant, though he be lord of all. But is under *tutors* and governors until the time appointed of the father." From this it appears, that the means of *instruction* were provided for *servants* as well as children; and indeed we know it must have been so among the Jews, because their servants were not permitted to remain in perpetual bondage, and therefore it was absolutely necessary they should be prepared to occupy higher stations in society than those of servants. Is it so at the South, my friends? Is the daily bread of instruction provided for your slaves? are their minds enlightened, and they gradually prepared to rise from the grade of menials into that of *free*, independent members of the state? Let your own statute book, and your own daily experience, answer these questions.

If this apostle sanctioned *slavery*, why did he exhort masters-thus in his epistle to the Ephesians, "and ye, masters, do the same things unto them (i.e. perform your duties to your servants as unto Christ, not unto me) forbearing threatening; knowing that your master also is in heaven, neither is there respect of persons with him." And in Colossians, "Masters give unto your servants that which is just and equal, knowing that ye also have a master in heaven." Let slaveholders only obey these injunctions of Paul, and I am satisfied slavery would soon be abolished. If he thought it sinful even to *threaten* servants, surely he must have thought it sinful to flog and to beat them with sticks and paddles; indeed, when delineating the character of a bishop, he expressly names this as one feature of it, "no striker." Let masters give unto their servants that which is *just* and *equal*, and all that vast system of unrequited labor would crumble into ruin. Yes, and if they once felt they had no right to the *labor* of their servants without pay, surely they could not think they had a right to their wives, their children, and their own bodies. Again, how can it be said Paul sanctioned slavery, when, as though to put this matter beyond all doubt, in that black catalogue of sins enumerated in his first epistle to Timothy, he mentions "*menstealers*," which word may be translated "*slavedealers*." But you may say, we all despise slavedealers as much as any one can; they are never admitted into genteel or respectable society. And why not? Is it not because even you shrink back from the idea of associating with those who make their fortunes by trading in the bodies and souls of men, women, and children? whose daily work it is to break human hearts, by tearing wives from their husbands, and children from their parents? But why hold slavedealers as despicable, if their trade is lawful and virtuous? and why despise them more than the gentlemen of fortune and standing who employ them as *their* agents? Why more than the professors of religion who barter their fellow-professors to them for gold and silver? We do not despise the land agent, or the physician, or the merchant, and why? Simply because their professions are virtuous and honorable; and if the trade of men-jobbers was honorable, you would not despise them either. There is no difference in *principle*, in Christian ethics, between the despised slavedealer and the *Christian* who buys slaves from, or sells slaves, to him; indeed, if slaves were not wanted by the respectable, the wealthy, and the religious in a community, there would be no slaves in that community, and of course no *slavedealers*. It is then the *Christians* and the honorable men and *women* of the South, who are the main pillars of this grand temple built to Mammon and to Moloch. It is the most enlightened in every country who are *most* to blame when any public sin is supported by public opinion, hence Isaiah says, "*When* the Lord hath performed his whole work upon mount *Zion* and on *Jerusalem*, (then) I will punish the fruit of the stout heart of the king of Assyria, and the glory of his high looks." And was it not so? Open the historical records of that age, was not Israel carried into captivity B.C. 606, Judah B.C. 588, and the stout heart of the heathen monarchy not punished until B.C. 536, fifty-two years *after* Judah's, and seventy years *after* Israel's captivity, when it was overthrown by Cyrus, king of Persia? Hence, too, the apostle Peter says, "judgment must begin at the house of God." Surely this would not be the case, if the professors of religion were not most worthy of blame.

But it may be asked, why are *they* most culpable? I will tell you, my friends. It is because sin is imputed to us just in proportion to the spiritual light we receive. Thus the prophet Amos says, in the name of Jehovah, "You *only* have I known of all the families of the earth: *therefore* I will punish *you* for all your iniquities." Hear too the doctrine of our Lord on this important subject; "The servant who *knew* his Lord's will and prepared not himself, neither did according to his will, shall be beaten with *many* stripes:" and why? "For unto whomsoever *much* is given, of him shall *much* be required; and to whom men have committed *much*, of *him* they will ask the *more*." Oh! then that the **Christians** of the south would ponder these things in their hearts, and awake to the vast responsibilities which rest upon them at this important crisis.

I have thus, I think, clearly proved to you seven propositions, viz.: First, that slavery is contrary to the declaration of our independence. Second, that it is contrary to the first charter of human rights given to Adam, and renewed to Noah. Third, that the fact of slavery having been the subject of prophecy, furnishes *no* excuse whatever to slavedealers. Fourth, that no such system existed under the patriarchal dispensation. Fifth, that slavery never existed under the Jewish dispensation; but so far otherwise, that every servant was placed under the protection of law, and care taken not only to prevent all *involuntary* servitude, but all voluntary perpetual bondage. Sixth, that slavery in America reduces a *man* to a *thing*, a "chattel personal," robs him of *all* his rights as a human being, fetters both his mind and body, and protects the *master* in the most unnatural and unreasonable power, whilst it throws him out of the protection of law. Seventh, that slavery is contrary to the example and precepts of our holy and merciful Redeemer, and of his apostles.

But perhaps you will be ready to query, why appeal to *women* on this subject? *We* do not make the laws which perpetuate slavery. *No* legislative power is vested in us; we can do nothing to overthrow the system, even if we wished to do so. To this I reply, I know you do not make the laws, but I also know that you are the wives and mothers, the sisters and daughters of those who do; and if you really suppose *you* can do nothing to overthrow slavery, you are greatly mistaken. You can do much in every way: four things I will name. 1st. You can read on this subject. 2d. You can pray over this subject. 3d. You can speak on this subject. 4th. You can *act* on this subject. I have not placed reading before praying because I regard it more important, but because, in order to pray aright, we must understand what we are praying for; it is only then we can "pray with the understanding and the spirit also."

1. Read then on the subject of slavery. Search the Scriptures daily, whether the things I have told you are true. Other books and papers might be a great help to you

in this investigation, but they are not necessary, and it is hardly probable that your Committees of Vigilance will allow you to have any other. The ***Bible*** then is the book I want you to read in the spirit of inquiry, and the spirit of prayer. Even the enemies of Abolitionists, acknowledge that their doctrines are drawn from it. In the great mob in Boston, last autumn, when the books and papers of the Anti-Slavery Society, were thrown out of the windows of their office, one individual laid hold of the Bible and was about tossing it out to the ground, when another reminded him that it was the Bible he had in his hand. "O! 'tis all one," he replied, and out went the sacred volume, along with the rest. We thank him for the acknowledgment. Yes, "it is all one," for our books and papers are mostly commentaries on the Bible, and the Declaration. Read the ***Bible*** then, it contains the words of Jesus, and they are spirit and life. Judge for yourselves whether he sanctioned such a system of oppression and crime.

2. Pray over this subject. When you have entered into your closets, and shut to the doors, then pray to your father, who seeth in secret, that he would open your eyes to see whether slavery is ***sinful***, and if it is, that he would enable you to bear a faithful, open and unshrinking testimony against it, and to do whatsoever your hands find to do, leaving the consequences entirely to him, who still says to us whenever we try to reason away duty from the fear of consequences, "What is that to thee, follow thou me." Pray also for that poor slave, that he may be kept patient and submissive under his hard lot, until God is pleased to open the door of freedom to him without violence or bloodshed. Pray too for the master that his heart may be softened, and he made willing to acknowledge, as Joseph's brethren did, "Verily we are guilty concerning our brother," before he will be compelled to add in consequence of Divine judgment, "therefore is all this evil come upon us." Pray also for all your brethren and sisters who are laboring in the righteous cause of Emancipation in the Northern States, England and the world. There is great encouragement for prayer in these words of our Lord. "Whatsoever ye shall ask the Father in my name, he will give it to you"--Pray then without ceasing, in the closet and the social circle.

3. Speak on this subject. It is through the tongue, the pen, and the press, that truth is principally propagated. Speak then to your relatives, your friends, your

acquaintances on the subject of slavery; be not afraid if you are conscientiously convinced it is ***sinful***, to say so openly, but calmly, and to let your sentiments be known. If you are served by the slaves of others, try to ameliorate their condition as much as possible; never aggravate their faults, and thus add fuel to the fire of anger already kindled, in a master and mistress's bosom; remember their extreme ignorance, and consider them as your Heavenly Father does the ***less*** culpable on this account, even when they do wrong things. Discountenance all cruelty to them, all starvation, all corporal chastisement; these may brutalize and ***break*** their spirits, but will never bend them to willing, cheerful obedience. If possible, see that they are comfortably and ***seasonably*** fed, whether in the house or the field; it is unreasonable and cruel to expect slaves to wait for their breakfast until eleven o'clock, when they rise at five or six. Do all you can, to induce their owners to clothe them well, and to allow them many little indulgences which would contribute to their comfort. Above all, try to persuade your husband, father, brothers and sons, that slavery is a crime against God and man, and that it is a great sin to keep human beings in such abject ignorance; to deny them the privilege of learning to read and write. The Catholics are universally condemned, for denying the Bible to the common people, but, slaveholders must not blame them, for ***they*** are doing the very same thing, and for the very same reason, neither of these systems can bear the light which bursts from the pages of that Holy Book. And lastly, endeavour to inculcate submission on the part of the slaves, but whilst doing this be faithful in pleading the cause of the oppressed.

> "Will ***you*** behold unheeding,
>   Life's holiest feelings crushed,
> Where ***woman's*** heart is bleeding,
>   Shall ***woman's*** voice be hushed?"

4. Act on this subject. Some of you own slaves yourselves. If you believe slavery is ***sinful***, set them at liberty, "undo the heavy burdens and let the oppressed go free." If they wish to remain with you, pay them wages, if not let them leave you. Should they remain teach them, and have them taught the common branches of

an English education; they have minds and those minds, ought to be improved. So precious a talent as intellect, never was given to be wrapt in a napkin and buried in the earth. It is the *duty* of all, as far as they can, to improve their own mental faculties, because we are commanded to love God with all our minds, as well as with all our hearts, and we commit a great sin, if we *forbid* or *prevent* that cultivation of the mind in others, which would enable them to perform this duty. Teach your servants then to read &c, and encourage them to believe it is their *duty* to learn, if it were only that they might read the Bible.

But some of you will say, we can neither free our slaves nor teach them to read, for the laws of our state forbid it. Be not surprised when I say such wicked laws ought to be no barrier in the way of your duty, and I appeal to the Bible to prove this position. What was the conduct of Shiphrah and Puah, when the king of Egypt issued his cruel mandate, with regard to the Hebrew children? "*They* feared *God*, and did *not* as the King of Egypt commanded them, but saved the men children alive." Did these *women* do right in disobeying that monarch? "*Therefore* (says the sacred text,) God dealt well with them, and made them houses" Ex. i. What was the conduct of Shadrach, Meshach, and Abednego, when Nebuchadnezzar set up a golden image in the plain of Dura, and commanded all people, nations, and languages, to fall down and worship it? "Be it known, unto thee, (said these faithful *Jews*) O king, that we will not serve thy gods, nor worship the image which thou hast set up." Did these men do right in disobeying the law of their sovereign? Let their miraculous deliverance of Daniel, when Darius made a firm decree that no one should ask a petition of any mad or God for thirty days? Did the prophet cease to pray? No! "When Daniel knew that the writing was signed, he went into his house, and his windows being *open* towards Jerusalem, he kneeled upon this knees three times a day, and prayed and gave thanks before his God, as he did aforetime." Did Daniel do right this to *break* the law of his king? Let his wonderful deliverance out of the mouths of lions answer; Dan. vii. Look, too, at the Apostles Peter and John. When the ruler of the Jews "commanded them not to speak at all, nor teach in the name of Jesus," what did they say? "Whether it be right in the sight of God, to hearken unto you more than unto God, judge ye." And what did they do? "They spake the word of God with boldness, and with great power gave the Apostles witness of the ***resurrection*** of the Lord Jesus;" although ***this*** was the very doctrine, for the preaching of which they had just been cast into prison, and further threatened. Did these men do right? I leave ***you*** to answer, who now enjoy the benefits if their labours and sufferings, in that Gospel they dared to preach when positively commanded not to teach any more in the name of Jesus; Acts iv.

But some of you may say, if we do free our slaves, they will be taken up and sold, therefore there will be no use in doing it. Peter and John might just as well have said, we will not preach the gospel, for if we do, we shall be taken up and put in prison, therefore there will be no use in our preaching. ***Consequences***, my friends, belong no more to ***you***, than they did to these apostles. Duty is ours and events are God's. If you think slavery is sinful, all you have to do is to set your slaves at liberty, do all you can to protect them, and in humble faith and fervent prayer, commend them to your common Father. He can take care of them; but if for wise purposes he sees fit to allow them to be sold, this will afford you an opportunity of testifying openly, wherever you go, against the crime of ***manstealing***. Such an act will be clear robbery, and if exposed, might, under the Divine direction, do the cause of Emancipation more good, than any thing that could happen, for, "He makes even the wrath of man to praise him, and the remainder of wrath he will restrain."

I know that this doctrine of obeying ***God***, rather than man, will be considered as dangerous, and heretical by many, but I am not afraid openly to avow it, because it is the doctrine of the Bible; but I would not be understood to advocate resistance to any law however oppressive, if, in obeying it, I was not obliged to commit ***sin***. If for instance, there was a law, which imposed imprisonment or a fine upon me if I manumitted a slave, I would on no account resist that law, I would set the slave free, and then go to prison or pay the fine. If a law commands me to sin I will break it; if it calls me to ***suffer***, I will let it take its course unresistingly. The doctrine of blind obedience and unqualified submission to any human power, whether civil or ecclesiastical, is the doctrine of despotism, and ought to have no place among Republicans and Christians.

But you will perhaps say, such a course of conduct would inevitably expose us to great suffering. Yes! my Christian friends, I believe it would, but this will ***not*** excuse you or any one else for the neglect of ***duty***. If Prophets and Apostles, Martyrs, and Reformers had not been willing to suffer for the truth's sake, where would the world have been now? If they had said, we cannot speak the truth, we cannot do what we believe is right, because the laws of our country or public opinion are against us, where would our holy religion have been now? The Prophets were stoned, imprisoned, and killed by the Jews. And why? Because they exposed and openly rebuked public sins; they opposed public opinion; had they held their peace, they all might have lived in ease and died in favor with a wicked generation. Why were the Apostles persecuted from city to city, stoned, incarcerated, beaten, and crucified? Because they dared to speak the truth; to tell the Jews, boldly and fearlessly, that ***they*** were the ***murderers*** of the Lord of Glory, and that, however great a stumbling-block the Cross might be to them, there was no other name given under heaven by which men could be saved, but the name of Jesus. Because they declared, even at Athens, the seat of learning and refinement, the self-evident truth, that "they be no gods that are made with men's hands," and exposed to the Grecians the foolishness of worldly wisdom, and the impossibility of salvation but through Christ, whom they despised on account of the ignominious death he died. Because at Rome, the proud mistress of the world, they thundered out the terrors of the law upon that idolatrous, war-making, and slaveholding community. Why were the martyrs stretched upon the rack, gibbetted and burnt, the scorn and diversion of a Nero, whilst their tarred and burning bodies sent up a light which illuminated the Roman capital? Why were the Waldenses hunted like wild beasts upon the mountains of Piedmont, and slain with the sword of the Duke of Savoy and the proud monarch of France? Why were the Presbyterians chased like the partridge over the highlands of Scotland--the Methodists pumped, and stoned, and pelted with rotten eggs--the Quakers incarcerated in filthy prisons, beaten, whipped at the cart's tail, banished and hung? Because they dared to ***speak*** the ***truth***, to ***break*** the unrighteous ***laws*** of their country, and chose rather to suffer affliction with the people of God, "not accepting deliverance," even under the gallows. Why were Luther and Calvin persecuted and excommunicated, Cranmer, Ridley, and Latimer burnt? Because they fearlessly proclaimed the truth, though that truth was contrary to public opinion, and the authority of Ecclesiastical councils and conventions. Now all this vast amount of human suffering might have been saved. All these Prophets and Apostles, Martyrs, and Reformers, might have lived and died in peace with all men, but following the example of their great pattern, "they despised the shame, endured the cross, and are now set down on the right hand of the throne of God," having received the glorious welcome of "well done good and faithful servants, enter ye into the joy of your Lord."

But you may say we are women, how can our hearts endure persecution? And why not? Have not women stood up in all the dignity and strength of moral courage to be the leaders of the people, and to bear a faithful testimony for the truth whenever the providence of God has called them to do so? Are there no women in that noble army of martyrs who are now singing the song of Moses and the Lamb? Who led out the women of Israel from the house of bondage, striking the timbrel, and singing the song of deliverance on the banks of that sea whose waters stood up like walls of crystal to open a passage for their escape? It was a ***woman***; Miriam, the prophetess, the sister of Moses and Aaron. Who went up with Barak to Kadesh to fight against Jabin, King of Canaan, into whose hand Israel had been sold because of their iniquities? It was a woman! Deborah the wife of Lapidoth, the judge, as well as the prophetess of that backsliding people; Judges iv, 9. Into whose hands was Sisera, the captain of Jabin's host delivered? Into the hand of a ***woman***. Jael the wife of Heber! Judges vi, 21. Who dared to speak the truth concerning those judgments which were coming upon Judea, when Josiah, alarmed at finding that his people "had not kept the word of the Lord to do after all that was written in the book of the Law," sent to enquire of the Lord concerning these things? It was a woman. Huldah the prophetess, the wife of Shallum; 2, Chron. xxxiv, 22. Who was chosen to deliver the whole Jewish nation from that murderous decree of Persia's King, which wicked Hannan had obtained by calumny and fraud? It was a ***woman***; Esther the Queen; yes, weak and trembling ***woman*** was the instrument appointed by God, to reverse the bloody mandate of the eastern monarch, and save the whole visible church from destruction. What Human voice first proclaimed to Mary that she should be the mother of our Lord? It was a woman! Elizabeth, the wife of Zacharias; Luke 1, 42, 43. Who united with the good old Simeon in giving thanks publicly in the temple, when the child, Jesus, was presented there by his parents, "and spake of him to all them that looked for redemption in Jerusalem?" It was a ***woman***! Anna the prophetess. Who first proclaimed Christ as the true Messiah in the streets of Samaria, once the capital of the ten tribes? It was a woman! Who ministered to the

Son of God whilst on earth, a despised and persecuted Reformer, in the humble garb of a carpenter? They were women! Who followed the rejected King of Israel, as his fainting footsteps trod the road to Calvary? "A great company of people and of *women*;" and it is remarkable that to them alone, he turned and addressed the pathetic language, "Daughters of Jerusalem, weep not for me, but weep for yourselves and your children." Ah! who sent unto the Roman Governor when he was set down on the judgment seat, saying unto him, "Have thou nothing to do with that just man, for I have suffered many things this day in a dream because of him?" It was a *woman!* the wife of Pilate. Although "he knew that for envy the Jews had delivered Christ," yet *he* consented to surrender the Son of God into the hands of a brutal soldiery, after having himself scourged his naked body. Had the *wife* of Pilate sat upon that judgment seat, what would have been the result of the trial of this "just person?"

And who last hung round the cross of Jesus on the mountain of Golgotha? Who first visited the sepulchre early in the morning on the first day of the week, carrying sweet spices to embalm his precious body, not knowing that it was incorruptible and could not be holden by the bands of death? These were *women!* To whom did he *first* appear after his resurrection? It was to a *woman!* Mary Magdalene; Mark xvi, 9. Who gathered with the apostles to wait at Jerusalem, in prayer and supplication, for "the promise of the Father;" the spiritual blessing of the Great High Priest of his Church, who had entered, *not* into the splendid temple of Solomon, there to offer the blood of bulls, and of goats, and the smoking censer upon the golden altar, but into Heaven itself, there to present his intercessions, after having "given himself for us, an offering and a sacrifice to God for a sweet smelling savor?" *Women* were among that holy company; Acts i, 14. And did *women* wait in vain? Did those who had ministered to his necessities, followed in his train, and wept at his crucifixion, wait in vain? No! No! Did the cloven tongues of fire descend upon the heads of *women* as well as men? Yes, my friends, "it sat upon each one of them;" Acts ii, 3. *Women* as well as men were to be living stones in the temple of grace, and therefore *their* heads were consecrated by the descent of the Holy Ghost as well as those of men. Were *women* recognized as fellow laborers in the gospel field? They were! Paul says in his epistle to the Philippians, "help those *women* who labored with me, in the gospel;" Phil. iv, 3.

But this is not all. Roman ***women*** were burnt at the stake, ***their*** delicate limbs were torn joint from joint by the ferocious beasts of the Amphitheatre, and tossed by the wild bull in his fury, for the diversion of that idolatrous, warlike, and slaveholding people. Yes, ***women*** suffered under the ten persecutions of heathen Rome, with the most unshrinking constancy and fortitude; not all the entreaties of friends, nor the claims of new born infancy, nor the cruel threats of enemies could make ***them*** sprinkle one grain of incense upon the altars of Roman idols. Come now with me to the beautiful valleys of Piedmont. Whose blood stains the green sward, and decks the wild flowers with colors not their own, and smokes on the sword of persecuting France? It is ***woman's***, as well as man's? Yes, ***women*** were accounted as sheep for the slaughter, and were cut down as the tender saplings of the wood But time would fail me, to tell of all those hundreds and thousands of ***women***, who perished in the Low countries of Holland, when Alva's sword of vengeance was unsheathed against the Protestants, when the Catholic Inquisitions of Europe became the merciless executioners of vindictive wrath, upon those who dared to worship God, instead of bowing down in unholy adoration before "my Lord God the ***Pope***," and when England, too, burnt her Ann Ascoes at the stake of martyrdom. Suffice it to say, that the Church, after having been driven from Judea to Rome, and from Rome to Piedmont, and from Piedmont to England, and from England to Holland, at last stretched her fainting wings over the dark bosom of the Atlantic, and found on the shores of a great wilderness, a refuge from tyranny and oppression--as she thought, but even here, (the warm blush of shame mantles my cheek as I write it,) even here, woman was beaten and banished, imprisoned, and hung upon the gallows, a trophy to the Cross.

And what, I would ask in conclusion, have ***women*** done for the great and glorious cause of Emancipation? Who wrote that pamphlet which moved the heart of Wilberforce to pray over the wrongs, and his tongue to plead the cause of the oppressed African? It was a ***woman***, Elizabeth Heyrick. Who labored assiduously to keep the sufferings of the slave continually before the British public? They were women. And how did they do it? By their needles, paint brushes and pens, by speaking the truth, and petitioning Parliament for the abolition of slavery. And what was the effect of their labors? Read it in the Emancipation bill of Great Britain. Read it, in the present state of her West India Colonies. Read it, in the impulse which has been given to the cause of freedom, in the United States of America. Have English women then done so much for the negro, and shall American women do nothing? Oh no! Already are there sixty female Anti-Slavery Societies in operation. These are doing just what the English women did, telling the story of the colored man's wrongs, praying for his deliverance, and presenting his kneeling image constantly before the public eye on bags and needle-books, card-racks, pen-wipers, pin-cushions, &c. Even the children of the north are inscribing on their handy work, "May the points of our needles prick the slaveholder's conscience." Some of the reports of these Societies exhibit not only considerable talent, but a deep sense of religious duty, and a determination to persevere through evil as well as good report, until every scourge, and every shackle, is buried under the feet of the manumitted slave.

The Ladies' Anti-Slavery Society of Boston was called last fall, to a severe trial of their faith and constancy. They were mobbed by "the gentlemen of property and standing," in that city at their anniversary meeting, and their lives were jeoparded by an infuriated crowd; but their conduct on that occasion did credit to our sex, and affords a full assurance that they will never abandon the cause of the slave. The pamphlet, Right and Wrong in Boston, issued by them in which a particular account is given of that "mob of broad cloth in broad day," does equal credit to the head and the heart of her who wrote it wish my Southern sisters could read it; they would then understand that the women of the North have engaged in this work from a sense of religious duty, and that nothing will ever induce them to take their hands from it until it is fully accomplished. They feel no hostility to you, no bitterness or wrath; they rather sympathize in your trials and difficulties; but they well know that the first thing to be done to help you, is to pour in the light of truth on your minds, to urge you to reflect on, and pray over the subject. This is all ***they*** can do for you, ***you*** must work out your own deliverance with fear and trembling, and with the direction and blessing of God, you can do it. Northern women may labor to produce a correct public opinion at the North, but if Southern women sit down in listless indifference and criminal idleness, public opinion cannot be rectified and purified at the South. It is manifest to every reflecting mind, that slavery must be abolished; the era in which we live, and the light which is overspreading the whole world on this subject, clearly show that the time cannot be distant when it will be done. Now there are only two ways in which it can be effected, by moral power or physical force, and it is for you to choose which of these you prefer. Slavery always has, and always will produce insurrections wherever it exists, because it is a violation of the natural order of things, and no human power can much longer perpetuate it. The opposers of abolitionists fully believe this; one of them remarked to me not long since, there is no doubt there will be a most terrible overturning at the South in a few years, such cruelty and wrong, must be visited with Divine vengeance soon. Abolitionists believe, too, that this must inevitably be the case if you do not repent, and they are not willing to leave you to perish without entreating you, to save yourselves from destruction; Well may they say with the apostle, "am I then your enemy because I tell you the truth," and warn you to flee from impending judgments.

But why, my dear friends, have I thus been endeavoring to lead you through the history of more than three thousand years, and to point you to that great cloud of witnesses who have gone before, "from works to rewards?" Have I been seeking to magnify the sufferings, and exalt the character of woman, that she "might have praise of men?" No! no! my object has been to arouse *you*, as the wives and mothers, the daughters and sisters, of the South, to a sense of your duty as *women*, and as Christian women, on that great subject, which has already shaken our country, from the St. Lawrence and the lakes, to the Gulf of Mexico, and from the Mississippi to the shores of the Atlantic; and will continue mightily to shake it, until the polluted temple of slavery fall and crumble into ruin. I would say unto each one of you, "what meanest thou, O sleeper! arise and call upon thy God, if so be that God will think upon us that we perish not." Perceive you not that dark cloud of vengeance which hangs over our boasting Republic? Saw you not the lightnings of Heaven's wrath, in the flame which leaped from the Indian's torch to the roof of yonder dwelling, and lighted with its horrid glare the darkness of midnight? Heard you not the thunders of Divine anger, as the distant roar of the cannon came rolling onward, from the Texian country, where Protestant American Rebels are fighting with Mexican Republicans--for what? For the re-establishment of *slavery*; yes! of American slavery in the bosom of a Catholic Republic, where that system of robbery, violence, and wrong, had been legally abolished for twelve years. Yes! citizens of the United States, after plundering Mexico of her land, are now engaged in deadly conflict, for the privilege of fastening chains, and collars, and manacles--upon whom? upon the subjects of some foreign prince? No! upon native born American Republican citizens, although the fathers of these very men declared to the whole world, while struggling to free themselves the three penny taxes of an English king, that they believed it to be a ***self-evident*** truth that all men were created equal, and had an unalienable right to liberty.

Well may the poet exclaim in bitter sarcasm,

>"The fustian flag that proudly waves In solemn mockery o'er a land of slaves."

Can you not, my friends, understand the signs of the times; do you not see the sword of retributive justice hanging over the South, or are you still slumbering at your posts?--Are there no Shiphrahs, no Puahs among you, who will dare in Christian firmness and Christian meekness, to refuse to obey the wicked laws which require woman to enslave, to degrade and to brutalize woman? Are there no Miriams, who would rejoice to lead out the captive daughters of the Southern States to liberty and light? Are there no Huldahs there who will dare to speak the truth concerning the sins of the people and those judgments, which it requires no prophet's eye to see, must follow if repentance is not speedily sought? Is there no Esther among you who will plead for the poor devoted slave? Read the history of this Persian queen, it is full of instruction; she at first refused to plead for the Jews; but, hear the words of Mordecai, "Think not within thyself, that ***thou*** shalt escape in the king's house more than all the Jews, for if thou altogether holdest thy peace at this time, then shall there enlargement and deliverance arise to the Jews from another place: but thou and thy father's house shall be destroyed." Listen, too, to her magnanimous reply to this powerful appeal; "I will go in, unto the king, which is ***not*** according to law, and if I perish, I perish." Yes! if there were but ***one*** Esther at the South, she ***might*** save her country from ruin; but let the Christian women there arise, at the Christian women of Great Britain did, in the majesty of moral power, and that salvation is certain. Let them embody themselves in societies, and send petitions up to their different legislatures, entreating their husbands, fathers, brothers and sons, to abolish the institution! of slavery; no longer to subject ***woman*** to the scourge and the chain, to mental darkness and moral degradation; no longer to tear husbands from their wives, and children from their parents; no longer to make men, women, and children, work without wages; no longer to make their lives bitter in hard bondage; no longer to reduce American citizens to the abject condition of ***slaves,*** of "chattels personal;" no longer to barter the image of God in human shambles for corruptible things such as silver and gold.

The women of the South can overthrow this horrible system of oppression and cruelty, licentiousness and wrong. Such appeals to your legislatures would be irresistible, for there is something in the heart of man which will bend under moral suasion. There is a swift witness for truth in his bosom, which will respond to truth when it is uttered with calmness and dignity. If you could obtain but six signatures to such a petition in only one state, I would say, send up that petition, and be not in the least discouraged by the scoffs and jeers of the heartless, or the resolution of the house to lay it on the table. It will be a great thing if the subject can be introduced into your legislatures in any way, even by ***women***, and ***they*** will be the most likely to introduce it there in the best possible manner, as a matter of ***morals*** and ***religion***, not of expediency or politics. You may petition, too, the different ecclesiastical bodies of the slave states. Slavery must be attacked with the whole power of truth and the sword of the spirit. You must take it up on ***Christian*** ground, and fight against it with Christian weapons, whilst your feet are shod with the preparation of the gospel of peace. And you are now loudly called upon by the cries of the widow and the orphan, to arise and gird yourselves for this great moral conflict, with the whole armour of righteousness upon the right hand and on the left.

There is every encouragement for you to labor and pray, my friends, because the abolition of slavery as well as its existence, has been the theme of prophecy. "Ethiopia (says the Psalmist) shall stretch forth her hands unto God." And is she not now doing so? Are not the Christian negroes of the south lifting their hands in prayer for deliverance, just as the Israelites did when their redemption was drawing nigh? Are they not sighing and crying by reason of the hard bondage? And think you, that He, of whom it was said, "and God heard their groaning, and their cry came up unto him by reason of the hard bondage," think you that his ear is heavy that he cannot ***now*** hear the cries of his suffering children? Or that He who raised up a Moses, an Aaron, and a Miriam, to bring them up out of the land of Egypt from the house of bondage, cannot now, with a high hand and a stretched out arm, rid the poor negroes out of the hands of their masters? Surely you believe that his aim is ***not*** shortened that he cannot save. And would not such a work of mercy redound to his glory? But another string of the harp of prophecy vibrates to the song of deliverance: "But they shall sit every man under his vine, and under his fig-tree, and none shall make them afraid; for the mouth of the Lord of Hosts hath spoken it." The ***slave*** never can do this as long as he is a ***slave***; whilst he is a "chattel personal" he can own ***no*** property; but the time is to come when ***every*** man is to sit under his own vine and his own fig-tree, and no domineering driver, or irresponsible master, or irascible mistress, shall make him afraid of the chain or the whip. Hear, too, the sweet tones of another string: "Many shall run to and fro, and ***knowledge*** shall be ***increased***." Slavery is an insurmountable barrier to the increase of knowledge in every community where it exists; slavery, then, must be abolished before this prediction can be fulfiled. The last chord I shall touch, will be this, "They shall not hurt nor destroy in all my holy mountain."

Slavery, then, must be overthrown before the prophecies can be accomplished, but how are they to be fulfiled? Will the wheels of the millennial car be rolled onward by miraculous power? No! God designs to confer this holy privilege upon ***man***; it is through ***his*** instrumentality that the great and glorious work of reforming the world is to be done. And see you not how the mighty engine of moral power is dragging in its rear the Bible and peace societies, anti-slavery and temperance, sabbath schools, moral reform, and missions? or to adopt another figure, do not these seven philanthropic associations compose the beautiful tints in that bow of promise which spans the arch of our moral heaven? Who does not believe, that if these societies were broken up, their constitutions burnt, and the vast machinery with which they are laboring to regenerate mankind was stopped, that the black clouds of vengeance would soon burst over our world, and every city would witness the fate of the devoted cities of the plain? Each one of these societies is walking abroad through the earth scattering the seeds of truth over the wide field of our world, not with the hundred hands of a Briareus, but with a hundred thousand.

Another encouragement for you to labor, my friends, is, that you will have the prayers and co-operation of English and Northern philanthropists. You will never bend your knees in supplication at the throne of grace for the overthrow of slavery, without meeting there the spirits of other Christians, who will mingle their voices with yours, as the morning or evening sacrifice ascends to God. Yes, the spirit of prayer and of supplication has been poured out upon many, many hearts; there are wrestling Jacobs who will not let go of the prophetic promises of deliverance for the captive, and the opening of prison doors to them that are bound. There are Pauls who are saying, in reference to this subject, "Lord, what wilt thou have me to do?" There are Marys sitting in the house now, who are ready to arise and go forth in this work as soon as the message is brought, "the master is come and calleth for thee." And there are Marthas, too, who have already gone out to meet Jesus, as he bends his footsteps to their brother's grave, and weeps, ***not*** over the lifeless body of Lazarus bound hand and foot in grave-clothes, but over the politically and intellectually lifeless slave, bound hand and foot in the iron chains of oppression and ignorance. Some may be ready to say, as Martha did, who seemed to expect nothing but sympathy from Jesus, "Lord, by this time he stinketh, for he hath been dead four days." She thought it useless to remove the stone and expose the loathsome body of her brother; she could not believe that so great a miracle could be wrought, as to raise that putrefied body into life; but "Jesus said, take *ye* away too stone;" and when *they* had taken away the stone where the dead was laid, and uncovered the body of Lazarus, then it was that "Jesus lifted up his eyes and said, Father, I thank thee that thou hast heard me," &c. "And when he had thus spoken, he cried with a loud voice, Lazarus, come forth." Yes, some may be ready to say of the colored race, how can *they* ever be raised politically and intellectually, they have been dead four hundred years? But *we* have **nothing** to do with **how** this is to be done; our business is to take away the stone which has covered up the dead body of our brother, to expose the putrid carcass, to show *how* that body has been bound with the grave clothes of heathen ignorance, and his face with the napkin of prejudice, and having done all it was our duty to do, to stand by the negro's grave, in humble faith and holy hope, waiting to hear the life-giving command of "Lazarus, come forth." This is just what Anti-Slavery Societies are doing; they are taking away the stone from the mouth of the tomb of slavery, where lies the putrid carcass of our brother. They want the pure light of heaven to shine into that dark and gloomy cave; they want all men to see *how* that dead body has been bound, *how* that face has been wrapped in the napkin of prejudice; and shall they wait beside that grave in vain? Is not Jesus still the resurrection and the life? Did he come to proclaim liberty to the captive, and the opening of prison doors to them that are bound, in vain? Did He promise to give beauty for ashes, the oil of joy for mourning, and the garment of praise for the spirit of heaviness unto them that mourn in Zion, and will He refuse to beautify the mind, anoint the head, and throw around the captive negro the mantle of praise for that spirit of heaviness which has so long bound him down to the ground? Or shall we not rather say with the prophet, "the zeal of the Lord of Hosts *will* perform this?" Yes, his promises are sure, and amen in Christ Jesus, that he will assemble her that halteth, and gather her that is driven out, and her that is afflicted.

But I will now say a few words on the subject of Abolitionism. Doubtless you have all heard Anti-Slavery Societies denounced as insurrectionary and mischievous, fanatical and dangerous. It has been said they publish the most abominable untruths, and that they are endeavoring to excite rebellions at the South. Have you believed these reports, my friends? have *you* also been deceived by these false assertions? Listen to me, then, whilst I endeavor to wipe from the fair character of Abolitionism such unfounded accusations. You know that *I* am a Southerner; you know that my dearest relatives are now in a slave Slate. Can you for a moment believe I would prove so recreant to the feelings of a daughter and a sister, as to join a society which was seeking to overthrow slavery by falsehood, bloodshed and murder? I appeal to you who have known and loved me in days that are passed, can *you* believe it? No! my friends. As a Carolinian I was peculiarly jealous of any movements on this subject; and before I would join an Anti-Slavery Society, I took the precaution of becoming acquainted with some of the leading Abolitionists, of reading their publications and attending their meetings, at which I heard addresses both from colored and white men; and it was not until I was fully convicted that their principles were entirely pacific, and their efforts only moral, that I gave my name as a member to the Female Anti-Slavery Society of Philadelphia. Since that time, I have regularly taken the Liberator, and read many Anti-Slavery pamphlets and papers and books, and can assure you I never have seen a single insurrectionary paragraph, and never read any account of cruelty which I could not believe. Southerners may deny the truth of these accounts, but why do they not *prove* them to be false? Their violent expressions of horror at such accounts being believed *may* deceive some, but they cannot deceive *me*, for I lived too long in the midst of slavery, not to know what slavery is. When I speak of this system, "I speak that I do know," and I am not at all afraid to assert, that Anti-Slavery publications have *not* overdrawn the monstrous features of slavery at all. And many a Southerner *knows* this as well as I do. A lady in North Carolina remarked to a friend of mine, about eighteen months since, "Northerners know nothing at all about slavery; they think it is perpetual bondage only; but of the depth of degradation that word involves, they have no conception; if they had, they would never cease their efforts until so **horrible** a system was overthrown." She did not know how faithfully some Northern men and Northern women had studied this subject; how diligently they had searched out the cause of "him who had none to help him," and how fearlessly they had told the story of the negro's wrongs. Yes, Northerners know *every* thing about slavery now. This monster of iniquity has been unveiled to the world, her frightful features unmasked, and soon, very soon will she be regarded with no more complacency by the American republic than is the idol of Juggernaut, rolling its bloody wheels over the crushed bodies of its prostrate victims.

But you will probably ask, if Anti-Slavery societies are not insurrectionary, why do Northerners tell us they are? Why, I would ask you in return, did Northern senators and Northern representatives give their votes, at the last sitting of congress, to the admission of Arkansas Territory as a state? Take those men, one by one, and ask them in their parlours, do you approve of slavery? ask them on **Northern** ground, where they will speak the truth, and I doubt not every man of them will tell you, *no!* Why then, I ask, did they give their votes to enlarge the mouth of that grave which has already destroyed its tens of thousands? All our enemies tell us they are as much anti-slavery as we are. Yes, my friends, thousands who are helping you to bind the fetters of slavery on the negro, despise you in their hearts for doing it; they rejoice that such an institution has not been entailed upon, them. Why then, I would ask, do they lend you their help? I will tell you, "they love the praise of men more than the praise of God." The Abolition cause has not yet become so popular as to induce them to believe, that by advocating it in congress, they shall sit still more securely in their seats there, and like the chief rulers in the days of our Saviour, though *many* believed on him, yet they did *not* confess him, lest they should be put out of the synagogue; John xii, 42, 43. Or perhaps like Pilate, thinking they could prevail nothing, and fearing a tumult, they determined to release Barabbas and surrender the just man, the poor innocent slave to be stripped of his rights and scourged. In vain will such men try to wash their hands, and say, with the Roman governor, "I am innocent of the blood of this just person." Northern American statesmen are no more innocent of the crime of slavery, than Pilate was of the murder of Jesus, or Saul of that of Stephen. These are high charges, but I appeal to their hearts; I appeal to public opinion ten years from now. Slavery then is a national sin.

But you will say, a great many other Northerners tell us so, who can have no political motives. The interests of the North, you must know, my friends, are very closely combined with those of the South. The Northern merchants and manufacturers are making *their* fortunes out of the produce of slave labor; the grocer is selling your rice and sugar; how then can these men bear a testimony against slavery without condemning themselves? But there is another reason, the North is most dreadfully afraid of Amalgamation. She is alarmed at the very idea of a thing so monstrous, as she thinks. And lest this consequence *might* flow from emancipation, she is determined to resist all efforts at emancipation without expatriation. It is not because she approves of slavery, or believes it to be "the corner stone of our republic," for she is as much *anti-slavery* as we are; but amalgamation is too horrible to think of. Now I would ask *you*, is it right, is it generous, to refuse the colored people in this country the advantages of education and the privilege, or rather the *right*, to follow honest trades and callings merely because they are colored? The same prejudice exists here against our colored brethren that existed against the Gentiles in Judea. Great numbers cannot bear the idea of equality, and fearing lest, if they had the same advantages we enjoy, they would become as intelligent, as moral, as religious, and as respectable and wealthy, they are determined to keep them as low as they possibly can. Is this doing as they would be done by? Is this loving their neighbor as themselves? Oh! that *such* opposers of Abolitionism would put their souls in the stead of the free colored man's and obey the apostolic injunction, to "remember them that are in bonds as bound with them." I will leave you to judge whether the fear of amalgamation ought to induce men to oppose anti-slavery efforts, when ***they*** believe ***slavery*** to be ***sinful***. Prejudice against color, is the most powerful enemy we have to fight with at the North.

You need not be surprised, then, at all, at what is said ***against*** Abolitionists by the North, for they are wielding a two-edged sword, which even here, cuts through the cords of caste, on the one side, and the bonds of interest on the other. They are only sharing the fate of other reformers, abused and reviled whilst they are in the minority; but they are neither angry nor discouraged by the invective which has been heaped upon them by slaveholders at the South and their apologists at the North. They know that when George Fox and William Edmundson were laboring in behalf of the negroes in the West Indies in 1671 that the very ***same*** slanders were propogated against them, which are ***now*** circulated against Abolitionists. Although it was well known that Fox was the founder of a religious sect which repudiated ***all*** war, and ***all*** violence, yet even he was accused of "endeavoring to excite the slaves to insurrection and of teaching the negroes to cut their master's throats." And these two men who had their feet shod with the preparation of the Gospel of Peace, were actually compelled to draw up a formal declaration that they were not trying to raise a rebellion in Barbadoes. It is also worthy of remark that these Reformers did not at this time see the necessity of emancipation under seven years, and their principal efforts were exerted to persuade the planters of the necessity of instructing their slaves; but the slaveholder saw then, just what the slaveholder sees now, that an ***enlightened*** population never can be a ***slave*** population, and therefore they passed a law that negroes should not even attend the meetings of Friends. Abolitionists know that the life of Clarkson was sought by slavetraders, and that even Wilberforce was denounced on the floor of Parliament as a fanatic and a hypocrite by the present King of England, the very man who, in 1834 set his seal to that instrument which burst the fetters of eight hundred thousand slaves in his West India colonies. They know that the first Quaker who bore a ***faithful*** testimony against the sin of slavery was cut off from religious fellowship with that society. That Quaker was a ***woman***. On her deathbed she sent for the committe who dealt with her--she told them, the near approach of death had not altered her sentiments on the subject of slavery and waving her hand towards a very fertile and beautiful portion of country which lay stretched before her window, she said with great solemnity, "Friends, the time will come when there will not be friends enough in all this district to hold one meeting for worship, and this garden will be turned into a wilderness."

The aged friend, who with tears in his eyes, related this interesting circumstance to me, remarked, that at that time there were seven meetings of friends in that part of Virginia, but that when he was there ten years ago, not a single meeting was held, and the country was literally a desolation. Soon after her decease, John Woolman began his labors in our society, and instead of disowning a member for testifying ***against*** slavery, they have for fifty-two years positively forbidden their members to hold slaves.

Abolitionists understand the slaveholding spirit too well to be surprised at any thing that has yet happened at the South or the North; they know that the greater the sin is, which is exposed, the more violent will be the efforts to blacken the character and impugn the motives of those who are engaged in bringing to light the hidden things of darkness. They understand the work of Reform too well to be driven back by the furious waves of opposition, which are only foaming out their own shame. They have stood "the world's dread laugh," when only twelve men formed the first Anti-Slavery Society in Boston in 1831. They have faced and refuted the calumnies at their enemies, and proved themselves to be emphatically peace men by never resisting the violence of mobs, even when driven by them from the temple of God, and dragged by an infuriated crowd through the Streets of the emporium of New-England, or subjected by ***slaveholders*** to the pain of corporal punishment. "None of these things move them;" and, by the grace of God, they are determined to persevere in this work of faith and labor of love: they mean to pray, and preach, and write, and print, until slavery is completely overthrown, until Babylon is taken up and cast into the sea, to "be found no more at all." They mean to petition Congress year after year, until the seat of our government is cleansed from the sinful traffic of "slaves and the souls of men." Although that august assembly may be like the unjust judge who "feared not God neither regarded man," yet it ***must*** yield just as he did, from the power of importunity. Like the unjust judge, Congress ***must*** redress the wrongs of the widow, lest by the continual coming up of petitions, it be wearied. This will be striking the dagger into the very heart of the monster, and once 'tis done, he must soon expire.

Abolitionists have been accused of abusing their Southern brethren. Did the prophet Isaiah *abuse* the Jews when he addressed to them the cutting reproofs contained in the first chapter of his prophecies and ended by telling them, they would be *ashamed* of the oaks they had desired, and *confounded* for the garden they had chosen? Did John the Baptist *abuse* the Jews when he called them "a generation of vipers" and warned them "to bring forth fruits meet for repentance?" Did Peter abuse the Jews when he told them they were the murderers of the Lord of Glory? Did Paul abuse the Roman Governor when he reasoned before him of righteousness, temperance, and judgment, so as to send conviction home to his guilty heart, and cause him to tremble in view of the crimes he was living in? Surely not. No man will *now* accuse the prophets and apostles of *abuse*, but what have Abolitionists done more than they? No doubt the Jews thought the prophets and apostles in their day, just as harsh and uncharitable as slaveholders now, think Abolitionists; if they did not, why did they beat, and stone, and kill them?

Great fault has been found with the prints which have been employed to expose slavery at the North, but my friends, how could this be done so effectually in any other way? Until the pictures of the slave's sufferings were drawn and held up to public gaze, no Northerner had any idea of the cruelty of the system, it never entered their minds that such abominations could exist in Christian, Republican America; they never suspected that many of the *gentlemen* and *ladies* who came from the South to spend the summer months in travelling among them, were petty tyrants at home. And those who had lived at the South, and came to reside at the North, were too ashamed of slavery even to speak of it; the language of their hearts was, "tell it *not* in Gath, publish it *not* in the streets of Askelon;" they saw no use in uncovering the loathsome body to popular sight, and in hopeless despair, wept in secret places over the sins of oppression. To such hidden mourners the formation of Anti-Slavery Societies was as life from the dead, the first beams of hope which gleamed through the dark clouds of despondency and grief. Prints were made use of to effect the abolition of the Inquisition in Spain, and Clarkson employed them when he was laboring to break up the Slave trade, and English Abolitionists used them just as we are now doing. They are powerful appeals and have invariably done the work they were designed to do, and we cannot consent to abandon the use of these until the *realities* no longer exist.

With regard to those white men, who, it was said, did try to raise an insurrection in Mississippi a year ago, and who were stated to be Abolitionists, none of them were proved to be members of Anti-Slavery Societies, and it must remain a matter of great doubt whether, even they were guilty of the crimes alledged against them, because when any community is thrown into such a panic as to inflict Lynch law upon accused persons, they cannot be supposed to be capable of judging with calmness and impartiality. We know that the papers of which the Charleston mail was robbed, were ***not*** insurrectionary, and that they were ***not*** sent to the colored people as was reported, We know that Amos Dresser was no insurrectionist though he was accused of being so, and on this false accusation was publicly whipped in Nashville in the midst of a crowd of infuriated ***slaveholders***. Was that young man disgraced by this infliction of corporal punishment? No more than was the great apostle of the Gentiles who five times received forty stripes, save one. Like him, he might have said, "henceforth I bear in my body the marks of the Lord Jesus," for it was for the truth's sake, he suffered, as much as did the Apostle Paul. Are Nelson, and Garrett, and Williams, and other Abolitionists who have recently been banished from Missouri, insurrectionists? We know they are ***not***, whatever slaveholders may choose to call them. The spirit which now asperses the character of the Abolitionists, is the very same which dressed up the Christians of Spain in the skins of wild beasts and pictures of devils when they were led to execution as heretics. Before we condemn individuals, it is necessary, even in a wicked community, to accuse them of some crime; hence, when Jezebel wished to compass the death of Naboth, men of Belial were suborned to bear ***false*** witness against him, and so it was with Stephen, and so it ever has been, and ever will be, as long as there is any virtue to suffer on the rack, or the gallows. ***False*** witnesses must appear against Abolitionists before they can be condemned.

I will now say a few words on George Thompson's mission to this country. This Philanthropist was accused of being a foreign emissary. Were La Fayette, and Steuben, and De Kalb, foreign emissaries when they came over to America to fight against the tories, who preferred submitting to what was termed, "the yoke of servitude," rather than bursting the fetters which bound them to the mother country? ***They*** came with carnal weapons to engage in ***bloody*** conflict against American citizens, and yet, where do their names stand on the page of History. Among the honorable, or the low? Thompson came here to war against the giant sin of slavery, not with the sword and the pistol, but with the smooth stones of oratory taken from the pure waters of the river of Truth. His splendid talents and commanding eloquence rendered him a powerful coadjutor in the Anti-Slavery cause, and in order to neutralize the effects of these upon his auditors, and rob the poor slave of the benefits of his labors, his character was defamed, his life was sought, and he at last driven from our Republic, as a fugitive. But was ***Thompson*** disgraced by all this mean and contemptible and wicked chicanery and malice? No more than was Paul, when in consequence of a vision he had seen at Troas, he went over to Macedonia to help the Christians there, and was beaten and imprisoned, because he cast out a spirit of divination from a young damsel which had brought much gain to her masters. Paul was as much a foreign emissary in the Roman colony of Philippi, as George Thompson was in America, and it was because he was a ***Jew*** and taught customs it was not lawful for them to receive or observe, being Romans, that the Apostle was thus treated.

It was said, Thompson was a felon, who had fled to this country to escape transportation to New Holland. Look at him now pouring the thundering strains of his eloquence, upon crowded audiences in Great Britain, and see in this a triumphant vindication of his character. And have the slaveholder, and his obsequious apologist, gained any thing by all their violence and falsehood? No! for the stone which struck Goliath of Gath, had already been thrown from the sling. The giant of slavery who had so proudly defied the armies of the living God, had received his death-blow before he left our shores. But what is George Thompson doing there? Is he not now laboring there, as effectually to abolish American slavery as though he trod our own soil, and lectured to New York or Boston assemblies? What is he doing there, but constructing a stupendous dam, which will turn the overwhelming tide of public opinion over the wheels of that machinery which Abolitionists are working here. He is now lecturing to ***Britons*** on American Slavery, to the ***subjects*** of a ***King***, on the abject condition of the slaves of a Republic. He is telling them of that mighty confederacy of petty tyrants which extends over thirteen States of our Union. He is telling them of the munificent rewards offered by slaveholders, for the heads of the most distinguished advocates for freedom in this country. He is moving the British Churches to send out to the churches of America the most solemn appeals, reproving, rebuking, and exhorting them with all long suffering and patience to abandon the sin of slavery immediately. Where then I ask, will the name of George Thompson stand on the page of History? Among the honorable, or the base?

What can I say more, my friends, to induce *you* to set your hands, and heads, and hearts, to this great work of justice and mercy. Perhaps you have feared the consequences of immediate Emancipation, and been frightened by all those dreadful prophecies of rebellion, bloodshed and murder, which have been uttered. "Let no man deceive you;" they are the predictions of that same "lying spirit" which spoke through the four hundred prophets of old, to Ahab king of Israel, urging him on to destruction. **Slavery** may produce these horrible scenes if it is continued five years longer, but Emancipation never will.

I can prove the *safety* of immediate Emancipation by history. In St. Domingo in 1793 six hundred thousand slaves were set free in a white population of forty-two thousand. That Island "marched as by enchantment" towards its ancient splendor, cultivation prospered, every day produced perceptible proofs of its progress, and the negroes all continued quietly to work on the different plantations, until in 1802, France determined to reduce these liberated slaves again to bondage. It was at this time that all those dreadful scenes of cruelty occured, which we so often *unjustly* hear spoken of, as the effects of Abolition. They were occasioned *not* by Emancipation, but by the base attempt to fasten the chains of slavery on the limbs of liberated slaves.

In Gaudaloape eighty-five thousand slaves were freed in a white population of thirteen thousand. The same prosperous effects followed manumission here, that had attended it in Hayti, every thing was quiet until Buonaparte sent out a fleet to reduce these negroes again to slavery, and in 1802 this institution was re-established in that Island. In 1834, when Great Britain determined to liberate the slaves in her West India colonies, and proposed the apprenticeship system; the planters of Bermuda and Antigua, after having joined the other planters in their representations of the bloody consequences of Emancipation, in order if possible to hold back the hand which was offering the boon of freedom to the poor negro; as soon as they found such falsehoods were utterly disregarded, and Abolition must take place, came forward voluntarily, and asked for the compensation which was due to them, saying, they preferred immediate emancipation, and were not afraid of any insurrection. And how is it with these islands now? They are decidedly more prosperous than any of those in which the apprenticeship system was adopted, and England is now trying to abolish that system, so fully convinced is she that immediate Emancipation is the safest and the best plan.

And why not try it in the Southern States, if it never has occasioned rebellion; if ***not*** a drop of blood has ever been shed in consequence of it, though it has been so often tried, why should we suppose it would produce such disastrous consequences now? "Be not deceived then, God is not mocked," by such false excuses for not doing justly and loving mercy. There is nothing to fear from immediate Emancipation, but every thing from the continuance of slavery.

Sisters in Christ, I have done. As a Southerner, I have felt it was my duty to address you. I have endeavoured to set before you the exceeding sinfulness of slavery, and to point you to the example of those noble women who have been raised up in the church to effect great revolutions, and to suffer for the truth's sake. I have appealed to your sympathies as women, to your sense of duty as Christian women. I have attempted to vindicate the Abolitionists, to prove the entire safety of immediate Emancipation, and to plead the cause of the poor and oppressed. I have done--I have sowed the seeds of truth, but I well know, that even if an Apollos were to follow in my steps to water them, "God only can give the increase." To Him then who is able to prosper the work of his servant's hand, I commend this Appeal in fervent prayer, that as he "hath chosen the weak things of the world, to confound the things which are mighty," so He may cause His blessing, to descend and carry conviction to the hearts of many Lydias through these speaking pages. Farewell-- Count me not your "enemy because I have told you the truth," but believe me in unfeigned affection,

Your sympathizing Friend,
Angelina E. Grimke.

THIRD EDITION.

[1] And again, "If a man be found stealing any of his brethren of the children of Israel, and maketh merchandise of him, or selleth him; then that thief shall die; and thou shall put away evil from among you." Deut. xxiv, 7.

[2] And when thou sendest him out free from thee, thou shalt not let him go away empty: Thou shalt furnish him ***liberally*** out of thy flock and out of thy floor, and out of thy wine-press: of that wherewith the Lord thy God hath blessed thee, shalt thou give unto him. Deut xv, 13, 14.

[3] There are laws in some of the slave states, limiting the labor which the master may require of the slave to fourteen hours daily. In some of the states there are laws requiring the masters to furnish a certain amount of food and clothing, as for instance, one quart of corn per day, or one peck per week, or one bushel per month, and "***one*** linen shirt and pantaloons for the summer, and a linen shirt and woolen great coat and pantaloons for the winter," &c. But "still," to use the language of Judge Stroud "the slave is entirely under the control of his master,--is unprovided with a protector,--and, especially as he cannot be a witness or make complaint in any known mode against his master, the ***apparent*** object of these laws may ***always*** be defeated." ED.

[4] See Mrs. Child's Appeal, Chap. II.

www.bookjungle.com email: sales@bookjungle.com fax: 630-214-0564 mail: Book Jungle PO Box 2226 Champaign, IL 61825

### The Codes Of Hammurabi And Moses
### W. W. Davies

QTY

The discovery of the Hammurabi Code is one of the greatest achievements of archaeology, and is of paramount interest, not only to the student of the Bible, but also to all those interested in ancient history...

*Religion*   **ISBN:** *1-59462-338-4*   *Pages:*132
*MSRP $12.95*

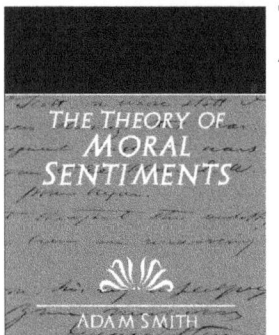

### The Theory of Moral Sentiments
### Adam Smith

QTY

This work from 1749. contains original theories of conscience amd moral judgment and it is the foundation for systemof morals.

*Philosophy*   **ISBN:** *1-59462-777-0*   *Pages:*536
*MSRP $19.95*

### Jessica's First Prayer
### Hesba Stretton

QTY

In a screened and secluded corner of one of the many railway-bridges which span the streets of London there could be seen a few years ago, from five o'clock every morning until half past eight, a tidily set-out coffee-stall, consisting of a trestle and board, upon which stood two large tin cans, with a small fire of charcoal burning under each so as to keep the coffee boiling during the early hours of the morning when the work-people were thronging into the city on their way to their daily toil...

*Childrens*   **ISBN:** *1-59462-373-2*   *Pages:*84
*MSRP $9.95*

### My Life and Work
### Henry Ford

QTY

Henry Ford revolutionized the world with his implementation of mass production for the Model T automobile. Gain valuable business insight into his life and work with his own auto-biography... "We have only started on our development of our country we have not as yet, with all our talk of wonderful progress, done more than scratch the surface. The progress has been wonderful enough but..."

*Biographies/*   **ISBN:** *1-59462-198-5*   *Pages:*300
*MSRP $21.95*

www.bookjungle.com  email: sales@bookjungle.com  fax: 630-214-0564  mail: Book Jungle  PO Box 2226  Champaign, IL 61825

### The Art of Cross-Examination
### Francis Wellman

QTY

I presume it is the experience of every author, after his first book is published upon an important subject, to be almost overwhelmed with a wealth of ideas and illustrations which could readily have been included in his book, and which to his own mind, at least, seem to make a second edition inevitable. Such certainly was the case with me; and when the first edition had reached its sixth impression in five months, I rejoiced to learn that it seemed to my publishers that the book had met with a sufficiently favorable reception to justify a second and considerably enlarged edition. ...

Reference    ISBN: *1-59462-647-2*    **Pages:412**    *MSRP $19.95*

### On the Duty of Civil Disobedience
### Henry David Thoreau

QTY

Thoreau wrote his famous essay, On the Duty of Civil Disobedience, as a protest against an unjust but popular war and the immoral but popular institution of slave-owning. He did more than write—he declined to pay his taxes, and was hauled off to gaol in consequence. Who can say how much this refusal of his hastened the end of the war and of slavery?

Law    ISBN: *1-59462-747-9*    **Pages:48**    *MSRP $7.45*

### Dream Psychology Psychoanalysis for Beginners
### Sigmund Freud

QTY

Sigmund Freud, born Sigismund Schlomo Freud (May 6, 1856 - September 23, 1939), was a Jewish-Austrian neurologist and psychiatrist who co-founded the psychoanalytic school of psychology. Freud is best known for his theories of the unconscious mind, especially involving the mechanism of repression; his redefinition of sexual desire as mobile and directed towards a wide variety of objects; and his therapeutic techniques, especially his understanding of transference in the therapeutic relationship and the presumed value of dreams as sources of insight into unconscious desires.

Psychology    ISBN: *1-59462-905-6*    **Pages:196**    *MSRP $15.45*

### The Miracle of Right Thought
### Orison Swett Marden

QTY

Believe with all of your heart that you will do what you were made to do. When the mind has once formed the habit of holding cheerful, happy, prosperous pictures, it will not be easy to form the opposite habit. It does not matter how improbable or how far away this realization may see, or how dark the prospects may be, if we visualize them as best we can, as vividly as possible, hold tenaciously to them and vigorously struggle to attain them, they will gradually become actualized, realized in the life. But a desire, a longing without endeavor, a yearning abandoned or held indifferently will vanish without realization.

Self Help    ISBN: *1-59462-644-8*    **Pages:360**    *MSRP $25.45* www.bookjungle.com *email: sales@bookjungle.com fax: 630-214-0564 mail: Book Jungle PO Box 2226 Champaign, IL 61825*

QTY

| | Title | ISBN | Price |
|---|---|---|---|
| ☐ | **The Rosicrucian Cosmo-Conception Mystic Christianity** by *Max Heindel* | ISBN: *1-59462-188-8* | **$38.95** |

*The Rosicrucian Cosmo-conception is not dogmatic, neither does it appeal to any other authority than the reason of the student. It is: not controversial, but is: sent forth in the, hope that it may help to clear...*
*New Age/Religion Pages 646*

☐ **Abandonment To Divine Providence** by *Jean-Pierre de Caussade*  ISBN: *1-59462-228-0*  **$25.95**
"The Rev. Jean Pierre de Caussade was one of the most remarkable spiritual writers of the Society of Jesus in France in the 18th Century. His death took place at Toulouse in 1751. His works have gone through many editions and have been republished...
*Inspirational/Religion Pages 400*

☐ **Mental Chemistry** by *Charles Haanel*  ISBN: *1-59462-192-6*  **$23.95**
Mental Chemistry allows the change of material conditions by combining and appropriately utilizing the power of the mind. Much like applied chemistry creates something new and unique out of careful combinations of chemicals the mastery of mental chemistry...
*New Age Pages 354*

☐ **The Letters of Robert Browning and Elizabeth Barret Barrett 1845-1846 vol II**  ISBN: *1-59462-193-4*  **$35.95**
by *Robert Browning* and *Elizabeth Barrett*
*Biographies Pages 596*

☐ **Gleanings In Genesis (volume I)** by *Arthur W. Pink*  ISBN: *1-59462-130-6*  **$27.45**
Appropriately has Genesis been termed "the seed plot of the Bible" for in it we have, in germ form, almost all of the great doctrines which are afterwards fully developed in the books of Scripture which follow...
*Religion/Inspirational Pages 420*

☐ **The Master Key** by *L. W. de Laurence*  ISBN: *1-59462-001-6*  **$30.95**
In no branch of human knowledge has there been a more lively increase of the spirit of research during the past few years than in the study of Psychology, Concentration and Mental Discipline. The requests for authentic lessons in Thought Control, Mental Discipline and...
*New Age/Business Pages 422*

☐ **The Lesser Key Of Solomon Goetia** by *L. W. de Laurence*  ISBN: *1-59462-092-X*  **$9.95**
This translation of the first book of the "Lernegton" which is now for the first time made accessible to students of Talismanic Magic was done, after careful collation and edition, from numerous Ancient Manuscripts in Hebrew, Latin, and French...
*New Age/Occult Pages 92*

☐ **Rubaiyat Of Omar Khayyam** by *Edward Fitzgerald*  ISBN:*1-59462-332-5*  **$13.95**
Edward Fitzgerald, whom the world has already learned, in spite of his own efforts to remain within the shadow of anonymity, to look upon as one of the rarest poets of the century, was born at Bredfield, in Suffolk, on the 31st of March, 1809. He was the third son of John Purcell...
*Music Pages 172*

☐ **Ancient Law** by *Henry Maine*  ISBN: *1-59462-128-4*  **$29.95**
The chief object of the following pages is to indicate some of the earliest ideas of mankind, as they are reflected in Ancient Law, and to point out the relation of those ideas to modern thought.
*Roligiom/History Pages 452*

☐ **Far-Away Stories** by *William J. Locke*  ISBN: *1-59462-129-2*  **$19.45**
"Good wine needs no bush, but a collection of mixed vintages does. And this book is just such a collection. Some of the stories I do not want to remain buried for ever in the museum files of dead magazine-numbers an author's not unpardonable vanity..."
*Fiction Pages 272*

☐ **Life of David Crockett** by *David Crockett*  ISBN: *1-59462-250-7*  **$27.45**
"Colonel David Crockett was one of the most remarkable men of the times in which he lived. Born in humble life, but gifted with a strong will, an indomitable courage, and unremitting perseverance...
*Biographies/New Age Pages 424*

☐ **Lip-Reading** by *Edward Nitchie*  ISBN: *1-59462-206-X*  **$25.95**
Edward B. Nitchie, founder of the New York School for the Hard of Hearing, now the Nitchie School of Lip-Reading, Inc, wrote "LIP-READING Principles and Practice". The development and perfecting of this meritorious work on lip-reading was an undertaking...
*How-to Pages 400*

☐ **A Handbook of Suggestive Therapeutics, Applied Hypnotism, Psychic Science**  ISBN: *1-59462-214-0*  **$24.95**
by *Henry Munro*
*Health/New Age/Health/Self-help Pages 376*

☐ **A Doll's House: and Two Other Plays** by *Henrik Ibsen*  ISBN: *1-59462-112-8*  **$19.95**
Henrik Ibsen created this classic when in revolutionary 1848 Rome. Introducing some striking concepts in playwriting for the realist genre, this play has been studied the world over.
*Fiction/Classics/Plays 308*

☐ **The Light of Asia** by *sir Edwin Arnold*  ISBN: *1-59462-204-3*  **$13.95**
In this poetic masterpiece, Edwin Arnold describes the life and teachings of Buddha. The man who was to become known as Buddha to the world was born as Prince Gautama of India but he rejected the worldly riches and abandoned the reigns of power when...
*Religion/History/Biographies Pages 170*

☐ **The Complete Works of Guy de Maupassant** by *Guy de Maupassant*  ISBN: *1-59462-157-8*  **$16.95**
"For days and days, nights and nights, I had dreamed of that first kiss which was to consecrate our engagement, and I knew not on what spot I should put my lips..."
*Fiction/Classics Pages 240*

☐ **The Art of Cross-Examination** by *Francis L. Wellman*  ISBN: *1-59462-309-0*  **$26.95**
Written by a renowned trial lawyer, Wellman imparts his experience and uses case studies to explain how to use psychology to extract desired information through questioning.
*How-to/Science/Reference Pages 408*

☐ **Answered or Unanswered?** by *Louisa Vaughan*  ISBN: *1-59462-248-5*  **$10.95**
Miracles of Faith in China
*Religion Pages 112*

☐ **The Edinburgh Lectures on Mental Science (1909)** by *Thomas*  ISBN: *1-59462-008-3*  **$11.95**
This book contains the substance of a course of lectures recently given by the writer in the Queen Street Hail, Edinburgh. Its purpose is to indicate the Natural Principles governing the relation between Mental Action and Material Conditions...
*New Age/Psychology Pages 148*

☐ **Ayesha** by *H. Rider Haggard*  ISBN: *1-59462-301-5*  **$24.95**
Verily and indeed it is the unexpected that happens! Probably if there was one person upon the earth from whom the Editor of this, and of a certain previous history, did not expect to hear again...
*Classics Pages 380*

☐ **Ayala's Angel** by *Anthony Trollope*  ISBN: *1-59462-352-X*  **$29.95**
The two girls were both pretty, but Lucy who was twenty-one who supposed to be simple and comparatively unattractive, whereas Ayala was credited, as her Bombwhat romantic name might show, with poetic charm and a taste for romance. Ayala when her father died was nineteen...
*Fiction Pages 484*

☐ **The American Commonwealth** by *James Bryce*  ISBN: *1-59462-286-8*  **$34.45**
An interpretation of American democratic political theory. It examines political mechanics and society from the perspective of Scotsman James Bryce
*Politics Pages 572*

☐ **Stories of the Pilgrims** by *Margaret P. Pumphrey*  ISBN: *1-59462-116-0*  **$17.95**
This book explores pilgrims religious oppression in England as well as their escape to Holland and eventual crossing to America on the Mayflower, and their early days in New England...
*History Pages 268*

www.bookjungle.com  email: sales@bookjungle.com  fax: 630-214-0564  mail: Book Jungle  PO Box 2226  Champaign, IL 61825

| Title | ISBN | Price | QTY |
|---|---|---|---|
| **The Fasting Cure** by *Sinclair Upton* — In the Cosmopolitan Magazine for May, 1910, and in the Contemporary Review (London) for April, 1910, I published an article dealing with my experiences in fasting. I have written a great many magazine articles, but never one which attracted so much attention... *New Age/Self Help/Health Pages 164* | 1-59462-222-1 | $13.95 | ☐ |
| **Hebrew Astrology** by *Sepharial* — In these days of advanced thinking it is a matter of common observation that we have left many of the old landmarks behind and that we are now pressing forward to greater heights and to a wider horizon than that which represented the mind-content of our progenitors... *Astrology Pages 144* | 1-59462-308-2 | $13.45 | ☐ |
| **Thought Vibration or The Law of Attraction in the Thought World** by *William Walker Atkinson* — *Psychology/Religion Pages 144* | 1-59462-127-6 | $12.95 | ☐ |
| **Optimism** by *Helen Keller* — Helen Keller was blind, deaf, and mute since 19 months old, yet famously learned how to overcome these handicaps, communicate with the world, and spread her lectures promoting optimism. An inspiring read for everyone... *Biographies/Inspirational Pages 84* | 1-59462-108-X | $15.95 | ☐ |
| **Sara Crewe** by *Frances Burnett* — In the first place, Miss Minchin lived in London. Her home was a large, dull, tall one, in a large, dull square, where all the houses were alike, and all the sparrows were alike, and where all the door-knockers made the same heavy sound... *Childrens/Classic Pages 88* | 1-59462-360-0 | $9.45 | ☐ |
| **The Autobiography of Benjamin Franklin** by *Benjamin Franklin* — The Autobiography of Benjamin Franklin has probably been more extensively read than any other American historical work, and no other book of its kind has had such ups and downs of fortune. Franklin lived for many years in England, where he was agent... *Biographies/History Pages 332* | 1-59462-135-7 | $24.95 | ☐ |

| | |
|---|---|
| **Name** | |
| **Email** | |
| **Telephone** | |
| **Address** | |
| **City, State ZIP** | |

☐ Credit Card     ☐ Check / Money Order

| | |
|---|---|
| **Credit Card Number** | |
| **Expiration Date** | |
| **Signature** | |

*Please Mail to:*  Book Jungle
PO Box 2226
Champaign, IL 61825
*or Fax to:*  630-214-0564

### ORDERING INFORMATION
**web**: www.bookjungle.com
**email**: sales@bookjungle.com
**fax**: 630-214-0564
**mail**: Book Jungle  PO Box 2226  Champaign, IL 61825
**or PayPal** to sales@bookjungle.com

*Please contact us for bulk discounts*

### DIRECT-ORDER TERMS

**20% Discount if You Order Two or More Books**
Free Domestic Shipping!
Accepted: Master Card, Visa, Discover, American Express

www.ingramcontent.com/pod-product-compliance
Lightning Source LLC
Chambersburg PA
CBHW081329040426
42453CB00013B/2356